BACKPACKI
THE CANADIAN I

HIGH SUMMER

By Chris Townsend

The Oxford Illustrated Press

ISBN 0 946609 63 2

Published by:
The Oxford Illustrated Press Limited, Haynes Publishing Group,
Sparkford, Nr Yeovil, Somerset BA22 7JJ, England.

Haynes Publications Inc, 861 Lawrence Drive, Newbury Park,
California 91320, USA.

Printed in England by:
J.H. Haynes & Co Limited, Sparkford, Nr Yeovil, Somerset.

British Library Cataloguing in Publication Data:
Townsend, Chris, *1949 –*
   High Summer: backpacking the Canadian Rockies.
   1. Canada.   Rocky Mountains.   Backpacking
   I. Title
   796.5'1'09711

Library of Congress Catalog Card No:
   89-83349

Contents

Acknowledgements

Without the generous assistance of all the following, the High Summer walk would not have been possible. Many thanks to them all.

First and foremost, John Traynor who put so much effort into organising the walk and who always believed I could do it, even when I phoned him up for help in the middle of the night! He also came up with the name 'High Summer'.

Sally Wood and the Canadian High Commission Tourism Section, P. Cavanaugh of Banff National Park, Ken Fisher of Kootenay National Park, Shirley Green of Yoho National Park, Kim Forster and Monika Schaefer of Jasper National Park, Karl Peck of Alberta Forestry, Wayne van Velzen of Mount Robson Provincial Park, F. Thiessen of the British Columbia Ministry of Forests and Lands, G. A. MacPherson of the British Columbia Ministry of Environment and Parks Outdoor Recreation Division and Ben Gadd for their help in the planning of the walk.

Maggie Hind and Wardair Canada for flying me and my supplies to Calgary.

Jane Marshall of Oxford Illustrated Press for risking giving me a book contract before I'd even planned the walk.

Karrimor International, Ski & Climb International, Phoenix Mountaineering, Field & Trek, Silva Compasses, RAB Down Equipment, Gregson First Aid Systems, Camera Care Systems and in particular Gordon Conyers of Craghoppers and Harald Milz of Enka (UK) for their support.

Ben and Cia Gadd for advice, hospitality and friendship; Chris and Janet Ainsworth, Denise and Rowena Thorn, Fran and Eleanor, Alain Kahan, Graham Huntington and especially my mother, Elizabeth Townsend, for the letters that kept me in touch with home; Diana Penny and Ang Zangbu for helping pack my supplies, Scott Steiner who first brought me to the Canadian Rockies, Stu Dechka, Sean Dougherty, Marc Salesse, Heather Smith, Marge Hage, Chris and Heather Collins, Butch

Osborne, Edna Acko, Jim Jackson, Theresa and Lewis Mull, Joel and Mary Roscl, Rabel J. Burdge, Hal Bleyhl, Alex Didow, Kerry Widsten, Irwin Hoppe, Mac and Gail McPherson, Rocky Notnes, Keith Bradley, Rick Foster, Bruce Dyer, Dave Dutton, Harv of Harv's Resort, Roy Richards, Harold and Mitsy Witmeir of Graham River Farm, Darwin Watson of Christina Falls Outfitting, Barry Tompkins of Big Nine Outfitters, Ross and Deborah Peck of Ross Peck Outfitters, Bill Woodhouse of the Parks and Outdoor Recreation Division in Fort St. John, John Bedell of British Columbia Forestry and all the other backpackers, outfitters, guides, hunters, foresters and people of the Canadian Rockies who helped me during the walk.

The Idea

'There is talk of doing a backcountry ski trip in the Canadian Rockies . . .'

It was the autumn of 1986 when I read those words in a letter from my American friend and wilderness companion, Scott Steiner. I'd first met Scott in southern California in 1982 on the Pacific Crest Trail when we'd gone through the snow-bound High Sierras together. Then in 1985 he'd accompanied me for the first month of my 3000-mile Continental Divide trek from Canada to Mexico along the Rocky Mountains. Both of these had been exciting and inspiring adventures and I was keen to go on more trips with Scott.

A flurry of letters back and forth across the Atlantic over the winter turned the 'talk' into reality and in the spring of 1987 I arrived in Banff townsite in the heart of the Canadian Rockies laden with Nordic ski mountaineering gear to meet Scott and the two others he'd recruited for our expedition, Todd Seniff and Clyde Soles. A ski along the high mountains in the four adjacent national parks of Banff, Jasper, Yoho and Kootenay was the idea, though our final plans had been left until we saw what the snow conditions were like. Our ski tour started with a crossing of the vast 125-square-mile Columbia Icefield, the biggest in the Rockies. This should have taken four days. Due to a week-long blizzard it took ten, several days being spent trapped in our tents by heavy snowfall and nil visibility. Battered by the storm we eventually skied out to the highway where Clyde hitch-hiked back to where we'd left his car. He was surprised when a car heading the other way turned round and offered him a lift.

The driver was Ben Gadd, an experienced mountaineer from Jasper townsite who'd guessed where Clyde had been as he'd done the same trip himself. Ben had also just written a comprehensive guide to the area entitled *The Handbook of the Canadian Rockies* and Clyde bought a copy. Crammed in the back of Clyde's car with rucksacks piled on my knee I glanced through this book as we headed for the luxuries of Banff, and alighted on the following:

'This leaves two great challenges, neither of which seems to have been accomplished yet. One is to hike the whole length of the Canadian Rockies . . . a distance of 1450km as the crow flies. It seems possible to do the whole hike in a summer.'

I felt a thrill of excitement as I read Ben Gadd's words and knew instantly that I would take up the challenge. Suddenly my main aim in life was to walk the length of the Canadian Rockies. Ever since I'd returned from walking from Canada to Mexico along the Continental Divide I'd been looking for another long wilderness walk to attempt. Over the years I've become attracted to wilder and remoter mountain country and what I saw of the Canadian Rockies made me realise that here was an ideal area for a major walk. Discovering that no-one had ever walked the whole length of these mountains was a bonus, offering an added edge of challenge to the undertaking.

To reach the end is not the reason for making such a trek though. Whilst having a goal helps to keep me going when I'm tired or the weather is bad, the real reason for such a walk is to live in the wilderness for a long enough period to feel at home there, to feel part of the natural world. That's why I usually go on my own, such a feeling being much harder to achieve when in the company, however congenial, of others. The Canadian Rockies seemed a perfect place to immerse myself in for a summer, a pristine mountain wilderness in which to wander.

The Setting

A great chain of mountains stretches for 2000 miles down western North America from northern British Columbia in Canada to Santa Fe in New Mexico in the USA: the Rocky Mountains. These are the first mountains the traveller from the east encounters as they tower dramatically above the vast prairies that lie in the heart of the continent. West of them lie range after range of mountains stretching all the way to the Pacific Ocean but these are not the Rockies; only the easternmost peaks make up that range. The Canadian Rockies are the northernmost 900 miles of the chain, running between 49 and 59 degrees of latitude (which in Europe would be from Plymouth to Oslo). The word 'chain' is appropriate as a description, for the Canadian Rockies are slightly less than 100 miles wide. Elevation ranges from 1000 feet at the junction of the Liard and Toad Rivers at the northern end of the range to the 12,972-foot summit of Mount Robson which is situated, appropriately for the high point, just about in the centre of the range.

Geologically the Rockies as a whole can be broken into several different groups. The Canadian Rockies, though, make up one integral range based on sedimentary rock which means that they have a consistent appearance throughout their length. This is most unusual in such a long chain of mountains and was one of the factors that made walking the length of the range in one trip so appealing. What better way to appreciate the integrity of these mountains than by travelling on foot from one end to the other? 'One can cross these mountains anywhere and recognize them immediately as the Canadian Rockies,' says Ben Gadd in *The Handbook*.

Three clear strands can be seen in the main mountain chain: the foothills on the eastern edge, then the Front Ranges and finally the Main Ranges, the highest peaks along which—as far north as the Peace River after which it wanders off to the west—runs the Great Divide, the watershed between the Atlantic and Pacific Oceans. I planned my route to include sections of all three regions. West of the mountains lies the great gash of the Rocky

Mountain Trench, a clear dividing line between the Rockies and the other mountain ranges of British Columbia.

Being far from the ocean the Canadian Rockies have a continental climate like the Alps, rather than a maritime one like the British hills. Ben Gadd quotes a climatological description (from the Koeppen system) of the region: a 'cold, snowy forest climate with no distinct dry season and short, cool summers'. This doesn't sound too promising but, as a walker used to British summer weather, I was to find the 'short, cool summer' to be quite hot and dry! High in the mountains though, snow can and does fall at any time of the year and freezing overnight temperatures are common, factors I needed to take into account in my planning.

Heavy glacial erosion has given rise to typical alpine topography with many large glaciers and icefields still remaining. Dense coniferous forests cloak the valleys and lower mountain slopes with timberline being around 7800 feet at the southern end, dropping to 5000 feet in the north. However as the mountain summits are several thousand feet lower in the north the general scale appears the same. The animal life is typical of a northern coniferous forest and mountain environment and includes grizzly and black bears, gray wolf, mountain lion, lynx, wolverine, beaver, mountain goat, bighorn sheep, caribou, moose (European elk), elk and more. The size of the wilderness still remaining untouched is such that these creatures can still flourish in a way that is impossible in most of the rest of the world.

Wilderness is a key word in describing the Canadian Rockies. Despite only 13% of the area being protected in parks most of the region is still untouched by development, unlike the American Rockies where small pockets of wilderness nestle uneasily against ski resorts, highways, mines, oilfields, towns and the other intrusions of modern society. Part of the reason for the unspoilt nature of the area is its remoteness, especially in the north where although there are few parks there are also few roads, towns and people. In the more easily accessible southern part lie the national and provincial parks, so much of the land here is being preserved. Soon though (within twenty years estimates Ben Gadd) unless far more of the area is brought under statutory protection the increasing encroachment of mining and forestry concerns into the wilderness will destroy the oneness of the Canadian Rockies and break it into small islands of protected land, unable to sustain the variety and volume of wildlife that the current vast unspoilt areas can.

Despite the essential oneness of the range I found the Canadian Rockies to divide neatly into two distinct sections. In the southern area of the well-known national parks are found the images which grace chocolate boxes, calendars, postcards and lavish picture books. Here are the famous Canadian Rocky scenes known the world over. With international airports at Calgary and Edmonton, excellent highway approaches, rail lines and bus services plus tourist towns offering every conceivable facility, the southern Rockies attract thousands of visitors every year. Even the backcountry is relatively crowded. There were few days in the mountain parks when I didn't meet other walkers. Groomed trails, bridged rivers, guidebooks, signposts, warden patrols and backcountry campsites with gravel tent pads, outhouses and picnic tables make backpacking in the mountains relatively easy. All this changes when you leave Jasper National Park half way up the range. Suddenly the tourists, the walkers and the facilities vanish. The small towns that exist are working towns, homes to miners, loggers, and hunters. Visitors are few and far between. Only a few outfitters and their clients ever venture far into the mountains. Hardly any trails exist and most of those that do aren't marked on the maps. This is frontier country. In the south I was just another walker, one of the many who walk the trails every summer. In the north walkers are a rarity and I attracted attention from everyone I met. My image of myself and what I was doing changed. In the south I was a backpacker on a long walk. In the north I felt more like an explorer.

The Planning

Once I was committed to the walk I had to think about the logistics, the details of which were to occupy me on and off from the moment I returned home from the ski trip in May 1987 until I started the walk itself thirteen months later. Most of the planning, like the writing of this book, was done on a word processor (nothing fancy or expensive, just an Amstrad PCW 8256) with reference literature piled up in a plastic box next to my desk. I ended up with a mound of letters and documents a foot high.

All my previous long walks, I'd planned on my own, which meant that I had missed many opportunities which as a self-employed outdoor writer and photographer (a professional backpacker if you like), I couldn't really afford to ignore. This time, though, a colleague, John Traynor, offered to act as 'manager' for the walk, which meant, for a change, that I didn't simply disappear for four months! John also took on the task of obtaining sponsorship for the trip which he carried out far better than I would have done. The actual cash costs of the trip slowly dwindled as everything from airline tickets to walking boots were obtained in exchange for promises of reports and pictures. The Canadian High Commission Tourist Department gave their support, as they had for the ski trip the year before, and provided all the maps plus a great deal of information. A contract for a book was obtained and an article by me about the walk appeared in *The Guardian*. This made obtaining support easier but also made me feel a little uneasy. I was sure this would be far and away the hardest walk I'd ever attempted. Was it wise to commit myself to writing a book before I'd walked a step? Writing about the walk in advance seemed to have a touch of hubris about it. Suppose I failed? Most of the time I managed to suppress such thoughts and keep my mind firmly on the practicalities of the planning. I had to believe I could succeed or I might as well not start. But sometimes I would wake in the dark and lie there wondering what I was committing myself to, doubts as to whether I really wanted to go ahead with the walk racing through my mind.

Long walks are actually made up of a series of shorter ones, the length of these determined by the whereabouts of places where food can be bought or sent to in advance and the weight of food that can be carried at one time. I find I need around 2lb dry weight of food a day, which means that a fortnight's food is the most I ever consider carrying and that's really too much when added to the weight of camping and walking gear. Before I could make decisions regarding supply points or even how long the trip would take, though, I needed a route. There being no obvious one nor, according to *The Handbook,* many trails in the northern half of the Rockies, planning that section would be the most difficult. Resupply there was a problem too, with no roads or towns anywhere near the mountains between Hudson Hope on the Peace River and the Alaska Highway nearly two hundred miles to the north.

In the south I'd be in the national and provincial parks most of the time with their good trails, prepared backcountry campgrounds and warden services, so route planning was easy—especially as much detailed information was available. With route planning in mind I'd bought a copy of Brian Patton and Bart Robinson's *The Canadian Rockies Trail Guide* before I'd left Canada in 1987. This proved indispensable. At the back of the guide were details of a proposed Great Divide Trail, intended to run from the border with the USA to Mount Robson, with a route plan for the national park belt. I decided to take this route as it looked an excellent high-level walk. The only long section in the south outside the parks was between Waterton Lakes National Park, where I would start, and Banff National Park. The Trail Guide listed a guide to this section published by The Great Divide Trail Association so I wrote to them requesting a copy. I never had a reply. The Forest Service recommended the same guide for a route through the area too, so I wrote again enclosing some money, again with no result. A route was supposed to have been partly built between Waterton and Banff but I could find no information as to its whereabouts and during the actual walk I saw no sign of it. In fact during the walk I never came across any mention of the Great Divide Trail at all, leading me to wonder whether the project has been abandoned.

I wrote to all the land management authorities for the whole of the Rockies to let them know of my plans and request information. All responded with advice and encouragement though those responsible for the northern half could offer little help. I wrote to Ben Gadd as well, partly to let him know his book had inspired someone to attempt the walk but mainly to ask his advice on a number of points. His reply was detailed and helpful, but again pointed out only problems for the northern half of the area: 'Resupply . . . will be either difficult or expensive, if not both . . . my advice: hire a helicopter and leave bear-proof caches at intervals'. He also outlined what would be the main hazards of the trip: 'river crossings . . . bear attacks . . . serious injury in isolated circumstances'. His advice to walk north rather than south, as I'd intended, in order to minimise the chances of encountering deep snow at the start (it melts later in the north) and to cross the unbridged northern rivers in late summer when they were low rather than in early summer when they'd be at their peak due to the snowmelt and glacier runoff, I accepted. The helicopter supply idea I took seriously enough to write a few letters of enquiry but abandoned it on finding out the cost: $500 to $600 (£250-300) per flight hour was way beyond my budget. Ben's suggestion that I contact the hunting outfitters who operate in the northern Rockies in the autumn, when I would be there, to see if they would take in my supplies to backcountry camps I didn't take up, which was a big mistake. Instead I took the simple choice, simple that is whilst sitting at home, of deciding to carry all my supplies from Hudson Hope to the Alaska Highway. If I could average around 18 miles a day, the section, I worked out, could be completed in 16 days, supplies for which I could just about carry. Of course I didn't know if I could average 18 miles a day in the trailless terrain of the northern Rockies. In fact I didn't know if I could average 6 miles a day. Finding out was one reason for going.

The long winter evenings of 1987/88 were spent poring over a set of 1:250,000 scale maps covering the whole of the Canadian Rockies working out the rough outline of a route. All I had when I began the planning were the start and finish points, namely the border with the USA and the Liard River, which marks the northern end of the Canadian Rockies. In *The Handbook* Ben Gadd says that geologically the southern boundary of what he calls the Canadian-style Rockies is at Marias Pass, sixty miles inside the USA, but as I had already walked that section as part of my Continental Divide walk I decided to walk north from the border. The other criterion I had for the route was that it was to be a wilderness one avoiding roads as much as possible. Once I had this outline I ordered the 79 1:50,000 topographic maps that it passed through. The maps of the southern half of the route were really only needed to provide more detail than the Trail Guide and to cover the short sections outside the parks. The northern ones, though, were essential, and across these I happily drew bold yellow lines, with no idea of whether I could be able to walk the route thus delineated or not! But with no detailed information on the area I had no choice. Wisely as it turned out I decided to take the larger scale maps with me as well in case I 'walked off' the more detailed ones.

Most of the planning for the second half of the walk was based on guesswork and minimal information. Rather than worrying I found this stimulating. The walk seemed to be splitting into two distinct parts. First a

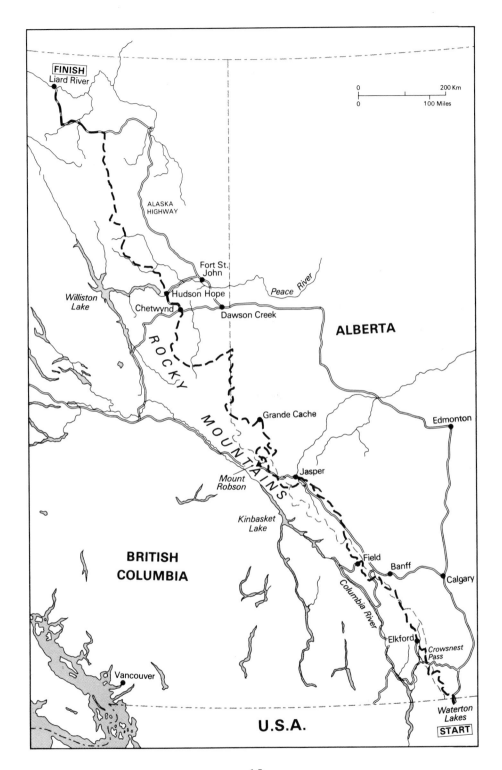

FINISH
Liard River

ALASKA
HIGHWAY

Fort St.
John

Peace River

Williston
Lake

Hudson Hope

Chetwynd   Dawson Creek

ALBERTA

R O C K Y

M O U N T A I N S

Grande Cache

Edmonton

Jasper

Mount
Robson

Kinbasket
Lake

BRITISH
COLUMBIA

Field
Banff

Calgary

Columbia River

Elkford

Crowsnest
Pass

Vancouver

Waterton
Lakes

U.S.A.

START

trail walk through the mountain parks which, whilst it would, I had no doubt, be enjoyable, would be like other walks I'd done in what I think of as 'planned' wilderness. I even had to apply for permits to camp in the backcountry and let the authorities know where I would be each night. Then would come the great unknown of the north. No-one would know where I was for possibly weeks at a time here. Was it possible to walk through that undeveloped wilderness? And could I, Chris Townsend, do it? What unforeseen problems would occur? It would be interesting discovering the answers to these questions.

My planning resulted in a 1500-mile route that I estimated would take 100 days to walk, very neat figures that I didn't believe for one minute. But at least they gave me a framework for the trip. Amazingly I ended up walking around 1600 miles in 124 days (of which 22 were 'rest' days), even though my actual route in the north bore little resemblance to my planned one.

As well as a route I needed gear and food (see the appendices for details). Choosing the former was not very difficult as I based my selection on previous experience and on the detailed knowledge of backpacking gear I've gained through years of testing items for magazines and manufacturers. Food was more of a problem as I'd never been totally happy with my choices on other long walks. Buying in bulk makes sense on a trip like this and I ended up trundling down to Halifax in my Panda 4x4 to visit the Suma wholefood warehouse. Here I purchased 100 days worth of dried food, loaded it into the back and trundled somewhat more slowly back to my home in the north-east.

All this had to be packed of course and shipped to Canada. I'd included eight supply points in my route to which provision boxes could be sent. Five of these were post offices, the others being Shirley Green of Yoho National Park in the town of Field, a backcountry ranger station in Mount Robson Provincial Park to which the park staff had kindly offered to transport my supplies, and Summit Lake Lodge on the Alaska Highway. The estimated times between each supply point ranged from five to sixteen days so each box would contain different amounts of food. One Sunday afternoon shortly before I left, John Traynor, Diana Penny and her husband Ang Zangbu of trekking company Bufo Ventures came over to help me pack. I'd prepared nine lists of food (one for supplies for the first section which I'd take with me) and placed these in empty boxes. A conveyor system was soon going as 10 kilo sacks of muesli and trail mix, tins of coffee and cartons of granola bars were broken down into the required quantities. Surprisingly it was all done in a few hours leaving me to add just camera film, maps and general odds and ends to each box before sealing it and addressing it to myself. Wardair had kindly agreed to freight the boxes to Calgary free of charge so they were sent off to Gatwick Airport by overnight transport.

The last weeks before my departure vanished in a rush of last minute details then suddenly it was too late to do any more and I was off to Gatwick with my huge rucksack. The long flight passed slowly and it was with impatient relief that I entered Canada and set off to retrieve my supply boxes from the customs shed. Two hours later I'd mailed them to myself! At the cargo shed manager Herb McGillevary said I should try the Yukon next. He'd been there once and for real wilderness that was the place. I had, I thought, better get this trip over before I started planning the next!

The final stage of my planning was to pick up my backcountry permits which I did at the Parks Canada office in central Calgary. After a night in a characterless, overheated hotel room I travelled to the Rockies by bus and taxi. The planning was over. Now the journey would begin.

Through Waterton Lakes National Park

Waterton Townsite to the Castle River
22nd to 26th June 55 miles

The walk began with a sense of *déjà vu* as I wandered around Waterton townsite just as I had done in 1985 at the start of the Continental Divide walk. I kept expecting to meet Scott Steiner walking down the street as had happened three years previously when he'd turned up to walk the first month south with me. Thinking of Scott was appropriate though due to his indirect involvement in this walk, his ski trip idea having brought me to the Canadian Rockies in the first place.

Waterton Lakes National Park is situated just north of the 49th Parallel which marks the border between the USA and Canada, which was where I wanted to start. The park is part of an International Peace Park along with Glacier National Park across the border. Founded in 1911, Waterton Lakes is the smallest of the Rocky Mountain national parks with an area of 203 square miles. The small size of the park has given rise to concern about its viability as mining, logging and tourist developments are encroaching on its edges. The fear is that the park is not big enough to sustain a full range of wildlife within its borders despite having Glacier National Park on its southern border.

The territories of animals such as bear, deer and elk spread outside the park into the forests on its border. It is these forests which are under threat. Much later in the walk I was to read a publication of the Alberta Wilderness Association entitled *Eastern Slope Wildlands: Our Living Heritage* which called for a 'buffer' circle of protected land around Waterton in order to keep the ecological diversity of the area intact. I was to find development within a few miles of the park's boundaries and I left the park sincerely hoping the area around it can be protected.

Waterton Lakes is also the least known and least accessible of the Rocky Mountain national parks. Further north I was to meet many people who'd never heard of it or had only a hazy idea of where it was. I

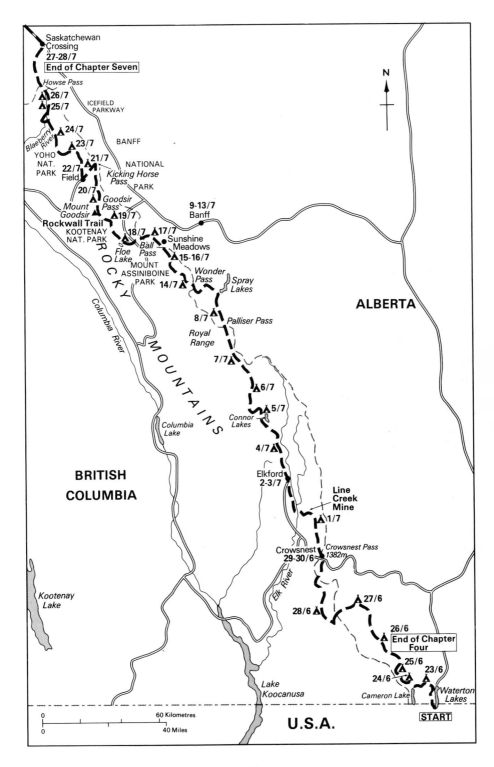

Saskatchewan
Crossing
27-28/7
☐ End of Chapter Seven

Howse Pass
▲ **26/7**
▲ **25/7**
ICEFIELD
PARKWAY
▲ **24/7**
Blaeberry River
▲ **23/7**
BANFF
YOHO
NAT.
PARK
▲ **21/7**
22/7 NATIONAL
Field
Kicking Horse Pass
20/7 ▲
▲ *Goodsir Pass*
PARK
9-13/7
Banff
Mount Goodsir
▲ **19/7**
Rockwall Trail
KOOTENAY
NAT. PARK
18/7 ▲ **17/7**
● Sunshine Meadows
Floe Lake
Ball Pass
▲ **15-16/7**
MOUNT
ASSINIBOINE
PARK
14/7 ▲
Wonder Pass
Spray Lakes

Columbia River

8/7 ▲ *Palliser Pass*
Royal Range

7/7 ▲

ALBERTA

▲ **6/7**
▲ **5/7**
Connor Lakes

Columbia Lake

4/7 ▲

Elkford
2-3/7

**BRITISH
COLUMBIA**

**Line
Creek
Mine**
▲ **1/7**

Crowsnest Pass
1382m
Crowsnest
29-30/6

*Kootenay
Lake*

Elk River

▲ **27/6**
28/6 ▲

26/6
▲ End of Chapter
Four

25/6
▲
24/6 ▲ **23/6**
Cameron Lake
Waterton
Lakes

*Lake
Koocanusa*

☐ **START**

0 ——————— 60 Kilometres
0 ——————— 40 Miles

U.S.A.

N

ROCKY MOUNTAINS

felt that by walking through it I was making up for the fact that in 1985 I'd started my Continental Divide walk here yet had left the park without seeing any of it beyond a few miles of lakeshore, which had seemed a peremptory way to treat such a beautiful place.

After checking into a room above a drapery store, recommended as cheap but convenient by the taxi driver who'd brought me the last few miles into the park, I dawdled in the small tourist town for a slow afternoon watching the crowds of summer which were just beginning to manifest themselves. As the sun began to set I ambled up the short, steep trail to a viewpoint directly above the town on the lump of rock known as the Bear's Hump. The sun dropped away behind the mountains, its last rays picking out the detail on the peaks that stretched out south into the USA above the dark waters of Upper Waterton Lake.

Next morning the 10 o'clock ferry took me and a crowd of others down the lake to the Goat Haunt Ranger Station in Glacier National Park, several miles inside the USA. The sun continued to blaze down from the sky and I noted the shade temperature of 28°C with disbelief before setting off on a 3½-hour walk back to the townsite along the 8-mile Lakeshore Trail. A riot of spring vegetation lined the path, the whites and purples of bear grass, dogwood, lupins, thimbleberry and more giving splashes of colour and light to the dark conifer forest. They also effectively hid the trail ahead and more particularly any animals which might be on it. Immediately on leaving the ranger station I'd encountered a rather lurid bear warning notice, a reminder, not that I needed one, of the presence throughout the Rockies of bears.

'The bear threat' can totally dominate and even ruin any trip into the Rockies if it is not countered with sensible precautions and, more importantly, an awareness of its true scale plus a degree of mental preparedness. Knowing I would be alone in bear country throughout the walk I'd tried to think myself into an accepting frame of mind in advance and to read what the experts had to say. The most reassuring passage, which I was to read several times during the walk, was Ben Gadd's: 'In 25 years on foot and unarmed in the mountains I have never been attacked by a bear . . . all the bears I have met on the trail, including grizzlies, have either run away or watched me curiously until I passed by.'

Two species of bear inhabit the Rockies: the black bear and the grizzly. Both are potentially dangerous if approached too closely (when they may attack because they feel threatened) and even more so if they have eaten human foods and learnt to hang around campsites in the hope of more. Most dangerous of all though are female grizzlies with young. Seventy per cent of known grizzly attacks have been by mothers with cubs. The reason seems to be that as male grizzlies will eat cubs if they can, the females have to be very protective.

Knowing the bears were always out there, maybe just round the next bend or behind the next bush, gave an edge to the walk, a sense of wildness, that walks in 'safer' terrain just do not have. Bears need vast amounts of space, their territories are huge. Their presence signifies the continuing existence of the wilderness. When they go, something is lost. And in much of North America they have gone, destroyed by the only creature more powerful than them: man. So trying to minimise the chances of a dangerous encounter with a bear was as much for the bears' sake as mine. Bears that become used to raiding camp sites lose their natural fear of people, after which a physical confrontation becomes almost inevitable with the bear often 'winning' the first round against an unarmed, unwary human being, but soon losing to the rifle bullets fired in retaliation.

The solution to camp bears, as they are known, is, luckily, simple. All food has to be hung up between two trees or else from a high branch. The minimum distances are twelve feet above the ground (the highest a grizzly can reach standing on its hind legs) and four feet away from the tree trunk and below any branch (in case a black bear tries to reach the food by climbing). I hung my food every night whatever the weather and whatever the time I made camp. This involved finding a suitable looking branch, then a rock to tie my cord round before hurling it over the branch, tying my food bags to one end and hauling them up in the air. If there were no large enough branches I would have to suspend the food between two trees which meant throwing each end of the cord over a branch and trying to ensure that the food bags ended up between the two. I soon learnt that some trees were much better than others. Large lodgepole pines were good, though smaller ones, densely packed together with thin, weak branches, were hopeless. Aspens were usually good too. Worst were the timberline firs and spruces with their short, downward curving branches designed for shedding snow. Sometimes hanging food was easy, sometimes it took several hours and had me shouting curses at the branches that broke and the rocks that came untied. However, whenever I felt I couldn't be bothered, I thought of a night-time visit from a bear and changed my mind. As it is the smell of food that attracts bears, I also slept well away from where I cooked and ate and never ever stored food in the tent, even for a moment.

Whilst walking, noticing any sign of wildlife becomes instinctive and I had no doubt once I'd been out a few days that I would respond quickly to any noise or movement. In fact the problem at first was that I overreacted, convinced that every rustle was a bear preparing to charge. Soon, though, I learnt to recognise the sounds made by different animals: the quiet shufflings of porcupines, the noisy explosion of sage grouse crashing through the bushes, the sharp click of deer hooves. Bears have poor eyesight but good hearing and an acute sense of smell. The chances were that a bear would be aware of me and keep out of my way without my even knowing it was nearby. Only when I was walking into a head wind and there was a lot of noise such as rushing water around was I likely to come across one unexpectedly. In those rare circumstances I shouted and sang and generally made my presence known. Mostly I did not do this, though, as it would have frightened off all the other wildlife as well. Indeed, on the few occasions when I was in thick vegetation with new bear signs such as pawprints and fresh droppings around and I blew my safety whistle loudly to warn the bears, the whole forest went absolutely quiet and an expectant pause ensued before life continued.

That first day I met no bears, though I did find some fresh dung on the trail. After four or so miles I came to Boundary Bay where the border lies between the USA and Canada. I paused here to think about my journey which really began in this small lakeside forest clearing beside the granite obelisk that marks the international border. North for 1000 miles stretched the Canadian Rockies, my home for the foreseeable future. I felt both exhilarated and not a little nervous at what lay ahead. So much was unknown. Could I really complete this walk?

A few miles further and I knew one thing for certain. I wouldn't finish the walk if I continued wearing the shorts I had on! They were already rubbing my thighs red, so once back in Waterton I purchased a new, looser pair. On a more serious note I wasn't finding my pack too comfortable either, even though I was only carrying a light day load and not the 65–85lb I'd have on my back for the rest of the walk.

Back in Waterton townsite I ate in the dark shadows of the Thirsty Bear Saloon and prepared my gear for the first week's backpacking. The next morning I enquired about the weather forecast. 'Between two systems', I was told. A few clouds dotted the sky but it was still very warm. I collected my permits from the trail office and was told my first grizzly story. Three days previously three hikers on the Rowe Lakes Trail, which I wanted to use, had been followed by a female grizzly with two cubs. They'd dropped their packs and run down to the highway. A ranger on horseback had then gone back up the trail and retrieved the packs, which the bear hadn't touched. Clearly she was defending her cubs rather than seeking food. The trail wasn't closed but caution was advisable, was the message from the rangers.

Having to use specific backcountry campsites in the national parks meant I had to plan my route and daily mileage around the positioning of these. As they weren't spaced at equal distances this resulted in some days being very short whilst others were rather too long. My first day out from the townsite was one of the former, as I climbed for just four miles and two hours to a fine 6100-foot timberline camp at Alderson Lake below the sheer 2200-foot-high cliffs and snow-patch-dotted scree slopes of Mount Alderson itself. The well-used site had a cooking shelter, outhouse and horse corral. I had it to myself though, apart that is from the wildlife. My presence immediately brought into the camp a variety of creatures used to scrounging food from visitors. Golden-mantled and Columbian ground squirrels darted around the site, trying to come in close without my seeing them, then dashing away if I turned in their direction. A couple of mule deer, so called for their large ears, wandered about, even coming into the shelter on one occasion. Various birds including American robins and pine grosbeaks nipped in and out of the camp for scraps. The small sub-alpine fir trees round about were not suited to hanging food and it took me two hours before I had my supplies out of reach of bears and the other animals.

A warm wind blew all night, gusting noisily in the trees and rattling the tent every now and then. I slept badly, each blast of wind waking me. Bears were present in my dreams and half-waking moments if not actually out there. It was to take a few more nights before I began to feel comfortable sleeping in bear country with no protection other than the thin nylon of the tent.

An 8am start saw me on a steep, twisting, open climb through beautiful alpine flower meadows (the first of many in the weeks to come), past Carthew Lake to the rocky, barren ridgeline of 7580-foot-high Carthew Summit and a spectacular view of 9400-foot Chapman Peak splashed with snow and towering over deep blue Lake Wurdeman. A perfect mountain scene. The wind on the ridge was cold and strong and I had far to go so I didn't linger, but soon began the long switchbacking descent down to Cameron Lake far below in the forest. I encountered many day hikers heading up and terrified one woman who flinched visibly as I came round a corner on the trail. 'I thought that was it, a bear was going to get me, when I heard you!' she said when she'd recovered herself enough to speak. She was wearing on her pack hipbelt the small 'bear bells' that many stores sell as deterrents—but I'd seen her before I'd heard them and I doubted they were loud enough to warn a bear of her presence. On this trail anyway there were so many people that any bears in the area would stay well away.

Cameron Lake is accessible by road so there were people everywhere, many of them scanning the avalanche slopes at the far end of the lake through binoculars. On enquiring the reason, I was told that several grizzlies with cubs had been seen feeding there. I had other bears to worry about as a short way up the road I would reach the Rowe Lakes trailhead and head up into the area where the three hikers had run into the grizzly family. I was pleased then to meet up with a young day hiker named Doug who wanted to go up to Rowe Lakes but like me was worried by the bear threat. Deciding that there was safety in numbers (and I felt less silly talking loudly with someone to talk to!) we travelled the trail together. Fresh droppings showed that the bears were still using the trail but we saw no other signs of them. The campsite was beautifully situated on the edge of the Rowe Basin meadows below the rock cirque of Mount Rowe. Unfortunately though the wooden outhouse had been placed right in line with one of the best views. Doug headed up for the summit whilst I set up camp, making a great deal of noise as I did so. Again there was no-one else there so I used one site for the tent and another for the kitchen, so any food smells would be well away from where I slept. Although the site was impressive the damp meadows meant there were rather too many mosquitos, a night-time problem that would grow worse over the next few months.

A strange loud rasping noise that seemed to be only inches from my ear had me awake and terrified in the middle of the night. I cautiously unzipped the tent door and peered out. A few feet away a mule deer stared back. It had been licking the tent, as it did several times more before dawn. I couple of times I even threw rocks at it in an attempt to drive it away. Then at dawn I found that my kitchen area had been thoroughly scoured by deer and the local squirrels. I'd left some socks and a bandana out to dry plus my walking stick which I'd leant against a tree. These were now strewn all over the meadow, half the bandana having been eaten! My stove and cookset had been upset and the dish cloth had vanished. As I wandered round picking up the scattered items I made a mental note not to leave anything out overnight in future. However, this upsetting start to the day was soon swept away by the fine high-level walking that followed, as I took the Tamarack Trail to Twin Lakes under the cliffs of the Great Divide, the watershed of North America.

Four days out though and certain problems were manifesting themselves. I had blisters on the palm of my hand from the walking stick and a sore spot on a toe, so these were plastered at lunchtime. As I set up a camera for a self-portrait the self-timer ceased working. I needed a self-timer in order to include myself in some of the scenes, many of which cried out for a figure in the foreground. Still—minor sores and blisters were expected in the first few days of the walk and the broken self-timer was no more than a nuisance. Much more worrying was my failure to adjust the pack to carry the load comfortably. I now had bruises on each hip and shooting pains across my shoulders. I wondered, momentarily, whether I was simply no longer up to carrying such weights but then I remembered that only a year previously I had carried an even heavier load for six weeks in a different model of the same pack with no problems. No,

24

it looked as though I would have to change to another pack very soon. Luckily, having had to buy new packs on previous long walks when the models I'd started out with eventually broke and knowing that being able to buy a pack once I was into the second half of the walk would probably be impossible without travelling a long way, I'd left a second pack along with other items that I might need with John Traynor, to be posted out if necessary.

The walking however was mostly very easy as the well-groomed trails were gently graded for uphills and every junction was signposted. Only where old avalanche debris lay across my route was there any difficulty. Crossing the tangle of ripped-down trees and hard packed snow of an uncleared avalanche chute could take a long time. In some places a swathe a hundred yards and more wide had been carved through the forest, the frightening power of tons of falling snow having crushed all that lay in its path. Later in the season, trail crews armed with axes and chain saws would clear a trail through the chaos but for now I had to fight a way across on my own. Branches, still a verdant green and full of sap, were trapped under tension in the jumble of compressed snow blocks that still remained. Poised on a hair trigger, the branches would spring up as I trod on them and I often found myself lying on my back, legs waving in the air, trying to extricate myself from my pack and struggle upright to continue my lurching balancing act across the network of torn-to-pieces trees.

So far I had met very few other people so it was pleasant to stop and chat to the ranger on horseback ('no bears around here') and the two backpackers (one in multi-coloured Hawaiian style shorts and shirt plus a vivid yellow pack) that I met that afternoon. Twin Lakes was another pretty campsite but the mosquitos were out in numbers so once I'd eaten I hid in the tent despite the temperature of 22°C. One other camper was there, his tent pitched right in the middle of a flower meadow next to the lake's outlet creek where it shouldn't have been—both according to park regulations and more importantly because it was crushing the fragile vegetation newly emerging after the winter. And from the point of view of comfort it would have been a damp site, replete with mosquitos. His food sack was hung a mere six or so feet above the ground a few yards away. I camped well away from him, deep in the woods, in the hope that if any bears did raid the camp they would ignore me.

Lying sweating in the tent I tried to work out my route for the next few days as I would leave the national park in a few miles and have no more maintained, signposted trails for a while. I was too hot and exhausted to come to any conclusions though. In fact I felt quite irritated and restless in the increasingly oppressive and humid atmosphere. Outside I could hear the click-click of mule deer hooves as several of them roamed nervously round the site. Just after 10pm the building storm broke with a distant rumble of thunder and light rain falling. A few minutes later and a strong wind blasted through the camp accompanied by heavy rain. Then the storm was overhead with continuous thunder and lighting. A loud crash reverberated from somewhere nearby in the forest. After half an hour the storm had passed, though the steady rain continued. It was much cooler and I soon fell asleep.

Dawn brought low cloud and more animal damage as I hadn't kept to my plan of protecting everything. Again a bandana hung out to dry had been molested as had my insulated jacket which had a hole torn out of the lining! On going down to the creek for water I came across the reason for the crash I'd heard. The storm had brought down a tall dead tree which lay across the trail right by the meadow where the other tent had been pitched. This was gone now, the owner having probably packed up and fled in the night as I'm sure I'd have done after such a near-miss. I was very glad I'd camped back in the woods and not out here in the open.

I left Waterton Lakes National Park at Castle Divide, a low point on a long east-west running ridge, and dropped down into the Castle River valley. Within a few yards of leaving the park I was on a bulldozed track which took me down to a dirt logging road. A moose, the first I'd seen, lumbered across the road in front of me. This, the largest member of the deer family, is called an elk in Europe which is very confusing as there is a North American elk, a close relation of the British red deer. On my first long walk in North America, the Pacific Crest Trail, I'd been confused by this nomenclature in the Oregon Cascades where other backpackers were surprised when I kept denying having seen any elk. It was some time before I realised the large deer I was seeing every day were elk. Moose are found throughout the Rockies and I was to see many of them during the walk. A creature of the Ice Age, designed for life in cold, snowy marshes, the moose is very distinctive with its long legs, hump and huge muzzle, meriting Ben Gadd's description of it as 'so ugly it is beautiful'.

Above the Castle River rose the impressive pinnacles and cliffs of Castle Peak and Windsor Mountain whilst beside me hurried the growing Castle River. Clear-cut areas marred the beauty though and became more frequent as the road became a stabilised gravel one with culverts and bridges. I followed a side track down to riverside meadows looking for a campsite but found only a devastated area with lots of rubbish including scraps of food strewn around so I bushwhacked along the bank to the next meadow which also showed signs of heavy usage by vehicle and horse parties with rustic wooden furniture and hitching rails spread about but no bear-attracting garbage. I camped in the woods but set up my kitchen on the meadow's edge with splendid views of the spires of North Castle peak.

Welcome to the Industrial Rockies

Castle River to Banff Townsite
27th June to 9th July   175 miles

The ramparts of North Castle hovered pale and insubstantial high above me in the drifting early morning clouds as I packed up camp ready to start my first long section outside the national parks. The first day showed the mixture of terrain that was to characterise travel in such areas. It began on a metalled road that soon became a graded gravel one which I left for a dirt track that took me down to the river. Rather than follow the road on a long curve to the east round the next wooded ridge running down from the main crest of the Rockies, an easy, unchallenging and boring option, I attempted to cut the corner by taking a direct line. Bushwhacking is the local term for off-trail travel in the forests and a most appropriate word it is, as I soon discovered as I thrashed along the river bank through the dense undergrowth. With a large and heavy pack to catch on every twig and branch, progress was slow. Eventually I forded the cold, knee-deep river to where my map showed a track on the far bank. The remnants of the track were there but it was very overgrown and almost impassable in places. As I struggled along, a thunderstorm blew in, showered me with rain and was gone in minutes. Cross-country ski trail signs appeared as I approached a road and lumber camp.

I crossed this gravel highway and climbed up another old track to a ridge beyond which lay the Carbondale River, my destination for the day. The track weaved this way and that and then headed off in the totally wrong direction, as so many were to do in the areas outside the parks, leaving me to bushwhack desperately for a few miles until I hit a forest road heading the right way. I barely glanced at the two coyotes that ambled across the road in front of me as I hammered down to the roaring Carbondale River to camp in the dense forest beside it. I had walked fifteen miles but it had taken me ten and a quarter hours and I was footsore, weary and thirsty. The blisters on my heel were throbbing and my legs stung with the scratches from all the bushwhacking. Clearly travel outside the parks was not going to be easy and I had to assume that tracks marked on the map might not turn out to be much use or even there at all. The pattern had been set for most of the next twelve days' walking.

An odd mixture of sounds greeted me the next morning as woodland bird song mingled with the deep bellowing of a large herd of cows. A few minutes after setting off I passed two dark green caravans and was greeted by a tumble of bodies bursting out of the door shouting 'what's your tribe then?' and laughing loudly. They turned out to be a forest service crew working on the rehabilitation of the area. Most of them were local Blood Indians but one, Jeff, was from eastern Canada and described himself as 'an African ten generations removed'. The 'what's your tribe then' phrase had been the Indians' humorous greeting to him when he'd arrived and it had now become their catchphrase, tried out on everyone they met. I stopped to chat as they were interested in what I was doing, hikers being uncommon here. Again a pattern for the walk was set. Whenever I was outside the mountain parks, which I was for over half the walk, anyone I met would be so surprised at encountering someone on foot that they'd want to know all about what I was doing. As I was always interested in the people and what *they* were doing in the Rockies this led to long conversations. Jeff was training to be a qualified forester and was very knowledgeable about trees and forest management techniques as well as being keen on conservation. Many of the eastern forests were ruined, he told me, but here in the west there was a chance of harvesting timber whilst still maintaining the woodlands. In this areas they were 'tidying up' the valley for its development as a provincial park.

Elvis, an Indian with magnificent long braids of hair, was interested in my being from Britain as his grandfather, a chief of the tribe, had travelled there as a member of a wild west road show many decades earlier, an episode he clearly regarded as a high point in his family history. He was still telling me about this when a work truck pulled up and they all piled in the back to head off for the site of the day's work.

I was heading west now for a high pass that would take me for the first time across the Great Divide, out of Alberta into British Columbia and onto the western slope of the Rockies where I would turn north again. Rain showers accompanied me as I followed a good track on a long rising traverse into the rocky defile of North Kootenay Pass. To the north the Flathead Range stretched grim and grey into the sheet iron sky. A plaque bolted to a rock slab told of how 'Thomas Blakiston, Gentleman and Explorer' had, in 1858, 'surveyed this historic Indian trail to determine its suitability as a rail route'. The Rockies were of course a major barrier to European expansion in North America and much effort went into finding ways across the range, firstly for fur traders to take their wares to the west coast ports such as Vancouver rather than all the way back across the continent to the east coast and then for roads and railways as the country became more developed. Surveying the narrow, steep-sided ravine myself I could see it was obviously totally unsuited to the latter purpose and in fact the railroad eventually went through Crowsnest Pass not many miles to the north which Blakiston didn't visit and about which he wrote, ironically, that it was 'a very bad road and seldom used'. Blakiston also named several local landmarks after prominent British naturalists including Waterton Lakes for Charles Waterton.

Approaching thunder and a strengthening cold wind soon had me racing down the far side of the pass to the cover of the forest which I reached just as a violent storm broke. The torrential rain, flashes of lightning and deafening thunder lasted throughout a complex and infuriatingly steep descent through a maze of abandoned logging roads. Once in the valley I made camp on a dismal, wet site beside Squaw Creek surrounded by devastated clear-cut land. Only two white-tailed deer bouncing through the debris lent any interest to the scene.

A long dirt-road slog through dense forest interspersed with logged clearings and, towards the end of the day, open-cast coal mines made the next day the least interesting so far. Apart, that is, from my having a companion for most of the time. At low, wooded Flathead Pass I caught a glimpse of something brown moving close behind me. I spun round in panic, thinking it was a bear, to see an alsatian dog looking plaintively at me. A closer look showed that she was starving, her bones protruding through her sodden coat. I stared at her wondering what to do. The look on her face told me that she regarded me as her saviour. She had a silver chain round her neck, though with no name on it, and I could only presume that she had somehow been left behind here and had been living in the woods ever since. We were a good ten miles or more from the nearest habitation and I had no food suitable for a dog—nor much food left anyway as I was near the end of my first section. In lieu of anything more suitable, I fed Flathead, as I named her due to a lack of any inspiration, some oatcakes and dried banana which she gulped down eagerly.

I realised how weak she was when I set off and found she couldn't keep up with me. Every hour or so I would stop and along she would come, slowly and painfully, to eat a few more oatcakes and totally overreact with gratitude to a few strokes on the head. Not that her weakness prevented her from making futile dashes at every squirrel she saw. Finally we reached the tiny mining community of Corbin where three women in a pick-up truck stopped and offered me a lift. I declined but explained about the dog which they agreed to take to an animal welfare centre they knew of in

Coleman, the town where they were going. As I watched them drive off I hoped that my friend for the day would find a happy home. I ended the day, after crossing back into Alberta over curiously named Ptolemy Pass, at the Kozy Knest Kabins which I found on the highway near Crowsnest Pass. Despite the appallingly cute name I checked in for two nights. Although I had only been walking for eight days and had only covered just over a hundred miles I needed a day off. My first planned supply point was still two or three days ahead and the blisters on my heels were very painful and getting worse and the pack was still bruising my hips. This was not a good start to the walk. I wrote in my journal: 'my feet have never been in such a state'.

A visit by taxi to the little mining town of Coleman saw me resupplied with moleskin, plasters, micropore tape, insect repellent and sunscreen, and unburdened of used maps and documents which were sent home and my fleece clothing which went ahead to Prince George to be collected in the autumn when temperatures would be lower. I hadn't worn it once and I could do with saving every ounce of weight. Coleman I found a rather sad, dispirited town showing clearly the decline of the coal industry in its general air of dilapidation. Coal mining began in the Crowsnest Pass area at the turn of the century after the Canadian Pacific Railroad laid tracks through the pass with the express purpose of exploiting the area's coal potential. Coleman was one of ten communities that sprang up to service the new industry. The local paper talked bravely of a coming economic recovery but seemed confused as to whether this would be based on coal (the new mines are in fact elsewhere), or tourism as did the town—which in places made a valiant if rather amateurish bid to lure visitors in. The most famous local attraction is the Frank Slide site. Here in 1903 some 36.5 million cubic metres of rock fell from Turtle Mountain and crushed part of the town of Frank killing over 76 people. I was more interested in the fine limestone block of Crowsnest Mountain that towers over the area. Crowsnest Pass itself is broad with gently sloping approaches, an obvious route through the mountains. I found it surprising it was discovered by white explorers so long after other higher and more difficult-to-reach passes. A plaque by the roadside on the pass tells the passer-by that it was 'long used by Indians but not shown on maps until the Palliser Expedition of 1860, and then only by hearsay'. The first trail across it was blazed by a Michael Phillips in 1873, fifteen years before the railway arrived. Given that local Indians had taken Thomas Blakiston to North Kootenay Pass thirty years earlier telling him that Crowsnest Pass was seldom used and not a good route, it seems as though they were deliberately keeping knowledge of the better route to themselves and thus slowing down the westward expansion of the white settlers. As this expansion was bringing in its train diseases such as smallpox to which the Indians had no resistance and which decimated their numbers, this was probably a wise, if in the long run futile, decision.

The first day north of Crowsnest Pass passed uneventfully on the highway and dirt roads, to end by Alexander Creek at an old hunters' camp depressingly littered with fire rings, tin cans and empty gun cartridges. I used it because it was the only flat spot around. A deer scuffling round the tent had me awake at 2.30am to watch a bright moon rising.

By dawn, clouds were sweeping across the pale sky. The dirt track wandered on through the forest and up to a high vantage point above the valley of Line Creek. My map showed the track continuing across the valley and up a ridge on the other side. I looked across the creek. There was no ridge, no mountain, no other side. Instead a huge open-cast coal mine sprawled black and threatening in front of me. The scale was shown by the tiny toy-like dumper trucks I could see emptying loads of debris down the giant slag heap opposite. Each load, tons of material in actuality, slid down the slope in a faint rumble to send up little puffs of dust as it reached the bottom. A road wriggled out west to the Line Creek gorge. I consulted my map. If I followed that road I should reach the gravel highway that led to the little town of Elkford, my first official supply point. It looked a long way. A half-uncontrolled slither down a steep logged hillside and a squelch through a nasty yellow, foul-smelling swamp took me to the creek, a quick paddle and the road. Beside it was an untended explosives dump and a Keep Out sign. I had an uncomfortable feeling that I wasn't meant to be here so I set off at a quick pace into a narrow, impressive cliff-rimmed ravine with barely space for the road. Sections were marked as in danger from avalanches during the winter. Blasts of rain and a chilling wind swept up the gorge forcing me to don my waterproofs. Once through the ravine I came to the mine entrance. A barrier was down across the road, and in the brightly-lit building beside it I could see a uniformed gatekeeper. Trying to sneak past unseen didn't seem very advisable as I was almost certain to be noticed so, deciding boldness was the best approach, I walked into the plush carpeted room and asked the startled occupant if I was on the right road for Elkford.

'How did you get in here? It's private property,' came the reply.

I explained. Clearly the mine authorities hadn't expected anyone to walk in by the back door, so to speak. I was directed down the road away from the mine. As I left I saw the guard reaching for the phone.

The day now became a forced march as I tramped up Highway 43 in the rain. A young moose bounded across the road in front of me. Any thoughts of stopping to camp were checked by the barbed wire fences and

31

No Trespassing notices lining the roadside. I reached Elkford at 8.30pm after a day of at least 25 miles with my feet in shreds and my back and shoulders throbbing. I staggered, dripping water everywhere, into the Elkford Motor Inn and was soon sitting in the dining room over a hot meal. It had been a long, long, long day and not one I wanted to repeat.

Even though it was only two days since I'd left Crowsnest Pass, my blistered feet needed another rest. I had to spend a day here anyway as I'd arrived on a Saturday and so couldn't collect my supply parcel from the post office until the Monday. In the meantime I had to do something about the pack. I phoned John Traynor in Newcastle after careful calculations as to the time difference. He took a long time in answering. 'You sound a bit sleepy,' I said. 'It *is* 1.30 in the morning,' he replied. 'Ah,' I said, 'Well, hm, sorry. I never was any good at arithmetic!' 'I was awake reading in bed, not asleep,' he said, which made me feel a little better. We arranged for my spare pack to be sent to Banff townsite, the next place I could collect it. My first photographs had arrived back and were, said John, OK though some self-portraits were a little underexposed. I also rang *Handbook* author Ben Gadd who'd asked me to contact him when I'd begun the walk as he'd like to walk some of it with me. I told him about the coal mine. 'Welcome to the Industrial Rockies,' he replied. I arranged to ring him again when I was nearer Jasper where he lived.

The Elkford Information Centre provided me with a map I needed for a route suggested in a letter from the BC Forest Service that had arrived just before I left England. I wished they'd told me about the Line Creek Mine. The proposed variant to my planned route looked good, requiring less road walking as it used trails not on the map but, said the letter, present on the ground. It also took me through the soon-to-be-designated Heights of the Rockies Wilderness Preserve. Elkford is a very small town and there isn't much to do there on a Sunday in the rain. The motel television provided old episodes of Dr Who, part of the Scott of the Antarctic drama series and highlights of Wimbledon. At least it was more interesting than staring at the walls.

In the café the next morning two locals told me that this area had the purest water and the most grizzlies in all the Rockies. The latter claim was one I heard everywhere. No-one else claimed they had the best water. I was more concerned with the discovery that Banff, my next supply point, was fifteen miles further away than I'd thought. Six not five days' walking in other words. And arrival on a Saturday again which meant another futile Sunday in town. I considered trying to do twenty miles a day. My aching body instantly protested and I knew I couldn't.

Three rivers were to take me to Banff National Park: the Elk, the White and the Palliser, linked by the crossing of high intervening ridges. A maintained River Walk with even a sign warning Steep Hill at the top of a stiff climb made for a gentle five miles out of Elkford. A big coal mine dominated the otherwise pretty views before a dense lodgepole pine forest closed in as I took to a dirt road. I had just despaired of finding anywhere to camp in the dense undergrowth and fallen trees beside the road when the Blue Lake Recreation Site materialised. Rain was falling so I stretched my nylon tarp over a picnic table using two trees, one tent peg, one bush and yards of cord to make a kitchen shelter. My walking stick and camera tripod helped hold the nylon above the table. A group of campavans and pick-ups was lined up at a nearby site. Amongst the people were some noisy kids and the usual mad axeman. On vehicle sites throughout western North America I've always seemed to encounter one of the latter. The steady thud of the axe goes on long into the night and signals the first rays of light long before the birds are singing. I always wondered what happened to all the unused wood that must be chopped up by these would-be woodsmen.

A faint glimpse of the peaks above the lake as the clouds shifted momentarily was all I had of a view as I began the climb to Connor Lakes on a rough trail. I was, I reflected, heading back into the wilderness again for the first time in eight days. Goodbye, thankfully, to the industrial Rockies. A sign by unbridged Quarrie Creek forbade motorised vehicles to go any further. I forded the creek in bare feet and plunged into the wet undergrowth. Soon afterwards I came across three bicycles lying against a fallen tree. I stared at them in disbelief. If they'd been mountain bikes it would have made some sense but as these were racing bikes I couldn't comprehend how they'd got here. I never met the owners so I never did find out. I found out why they'd not been taken any further though as I came upon a very rickety string-and-branch bridge suspended precarious- ly high above a creek. I scrambled down the bank and waded through the shallow water rather than trust the structure. My feet were already wet anyway. Waterfalls crashed down the deep gorge of Forsyth Creek as I approached Connor Lakes. Then out of the grey sky a huge magnificent bird appeared soaring low over the lake's surface right in front of me. It was a bald eagle, the first I'd seen. The shores of the bigger of the two Connor Lakes gave me the choice of four horse/angler camps. All were in varying degrees of dilapidation and squalor so I gave them all a miss and headed for the far end of the lake, after a false start as my map showed the trail on the wrong bank. I could see three anglers in a small boat near the far shore and wondered if they were the owners of the bicycles I'd passed. A cleaner site appeared at the north-west end of the lake so I stopped to set up camp. Immediately I started shivering and had to don all my clothes. I pitched the tarp and huddled under it. The temperature was a reasonable

12°C but the air was damp and there was a cooling breeze. Once I'd lit the stove and had a hot meal and a few hot drinks inside me I felt quite comfortable again.

Rain through the night had turned to snow by 9am. A very wet cold day ensued as I plodded up to a high pass and then down on a trail that kept vanishing and reappearing in the sodden forest to the sadly clear-cut Maiyuk Creek valley. Here I had difficulty fording the raging creek which was full of snowmelt and rain, but finally found a place where I could cling onto a fallen tree for most of the way across, using it as a barrier to prevent my being washed downstream. Logging roads then led to the wide White River valley and a bridge over the rushing stream. It took me an hour to find the unmarked trailhead for the path up the valley that the Forest Service had told me existed. Although it wasn't marked on my 1:50,000 map I finally located it after thinking to consult a 1:125,000 map that I'd bought in Elkford that did have it on. This map showed it to be farther away from the river than I'd guessed it to be. The trail's location was confirmed on seeing a horse party leaving a pick-up parked at a bend in the road. Beside the truck I found the still warm embers of a fire and the start of an excellent if muddy trail that took me in the horses' tracks to a camp in a grove of trees in the middle of some extensive riverside meadows with views upstream to rock spires and snowfields vanishing into the clouds. Although the weather had stayed grey and damp with fresh snow on the ground and steady drizzle falling and I'd had to wear my waterproofs all day, a couple of wildlife sightings had lifted what would otherwise have been a dismal day. In a clear-cut I'd seen the first elk of the walk, a whole herd of them that raced away on seeing me. Then by the White River I'd spotted a smaller white-tailed deer, a species easily identifiable by the white patch revealed under its uplifted tail when it runs.

I was camped not far away from the horse party I'd been following. From the far side of the meadow I could hear horses neighing and people shouting as well as a coyote howling. The cool, breezy weather made me regret sending my fleece garments on ahead from Coleman. The evening, thankfully, was dry and calm, though with dark clouds pouring across the sky from the west. These were the last clouds for a while as the storm had broken, and sunshine greeted me the next morning and I was soon back in shorts and tee shirt. Good if wet and muddy trails led me all the way to the Palliser River. Dominating the first part of the day were the peaks of the magnificent eastern wall of the White River valley, Mounts Abruzzi, Cadora, Swidenski and Joffre. With their huge, fresh snow-spattered cliffs they looked impressive, both from the valley and from above-timberline Sylvan Pass. From the latter a steep 3000-foot descent beside the torrent of Joffre Creek led down to the Palliser River, a descent that gave good views across glacial-debris-bottomed avalanche chutes to the continuing mountain ramparts from Joffre to Northover and over the Palliser valley to the white summits of the Royal Range, named after members of the British royal family. The scenery was the best I'd seen since leaving Waterton Lakes National Park. I also followed fresh bear prints all the way down and so kept a close look out for any sign of movement ahead. Camp was in a small, buggy, marshy meadow beside the river. During the day my left ankle had become swollen and discoloured and I'd wrapped a crepe bandage round it. The pain had eased as the day went on but the swelling was still there. Hanging my food was difficult due to the lack of decent-sized stones in the damp grass. The small pebbles I did find were not heavy enough, one of them spinning round a branch and becoming irretrievable along with a section of my cord.

A heavy dew left the tent soaked inside and out but it soon dried in the hot sun of the next morning. At 1.30pm the temperature in the open was 36°C! The hot day was welcome though as I found the easiest way to travel up the trailless, heavily forested valley was in the wide, braided Palliser River itself, using shingle banks where possible but spending much time wading through the cold, fast ankle-to-knee deep water. Progress was slow but enjoyable, with excellent views up ahead to a vast cirque nestled between Mounts Cradock and Back and to the east the huge monoliths of Defender and Onslow Mountains. As the valley began to grow narrower and steeper and the river faster, deeper and single-channelled, I came upon the empty locked cabins of the Palliser Guides' and Outfitters' Wilderness Camp beyond which a trail led up towards 6,900-foot Palliser Pass. A hand-written sign on the main cabin wall read 'Do not break into this cabin unless of (sic) an emergency. If you do not come to the mountains prepared you do not deserve to be in them.'

Two tricky stream fords were necessary beyond the cabins and during the second one, of Tipperary Creek, I slipped and went in crutch deep before I managed with a burst of fear-inspired adrenaline to haul myself out onto a boulder. Shortly before, I'd been admiring the waterfall I could see away to the west, high up on the mountainside pouring into Tipperary Cirque, little knowing I would have to ford the resulting torrent. The trail then faded out leaving me with a strenuous thrash up three thousand feet of dense vegetation to the pass and entry into Banff National Park. The shade temperature was 31°C and I stopped several times to fill my water bottle in the creek. On one occasion I dropped the cap into the water and watched as it sped away downstream. I turned away then something made me wade into the water to search for it. Amazingly I found it wedged against a rock.

Palliser Pass I found a confusing place. I thought I was there twice before I actually reached the highest point and began to descend. The Banff National Park boundary marker was not on the pass either, as I'd expected, but a little way down the far side. Once I reached it, however, the pass seemed a good omen to mark my re-entry to 'the national park backcountry trail system.

As I descended the upper Spray River valley I met a hiker with a camera on a tripod heading up to the pass. We greeted each other in passing. I then realised he was the first person I'd seen in five days. Back in a park I now had to use official backcountry campsites again. The Banff ones have numbers rather than names and I was booked into US10. However US14 turned up first and, as it was late and I was tired and there was no-one else there, I stopped and made camp. The site had the worst mosquitos yet but in recompense there was a cable and pulley system for hanging food. This made the procedure simple as all it involved was attaching the food bags to a large hook at the end of a strong wire cable, then hauling the load up via a pulley until it was twenty or so feet above the ground, dangling below a metal pole slung between two trees. This was my first encounter with such devices and I was very pleased to find them, as I was becoming fed up with the time-consuming process of hanging my food myself and was quite happy to have a respite from it. As such cables or similar are found throughout the parks I knew that for the next month or so I would be able to hang my food quickly and easily at every camp. US14 was situated in a small grove of trees on the western edge of the Spray River meadows across which I was able to see the bright pink of alpenglow on Mounts Sir Douglas and Leman, a fine display that had me reaching for my camera and tripod despite my weariness. My only campsite visitors were two porcupines which persisted in trying to grab my boots and other items until I chased them off.

The dawn mosquito hordes had me up and away early for a pleasant walk down the Spray River valley to Spray Reservoir. As I approached the roadhead at the reservoir I met several other people making an early start including two anglers heading up for a day's trout fishing, and two Australian backpackers who were heading for Mount Assiniboine Provincial Park, my next destination. First though I had to get to Banff townsite and pick up my supply box and replacement pack. My original plan had been to continue on through Assiniboine Park to the Sunshine Meadows ski area and take the gondola down to the road and then a bus to Banff, but that meant at least another two days' walking before I could change packs and I wanted to do that as soon as possible. I lunched by Watridge Lake where I talked to a Calgary woman out with her family on a fishing trip. Once at the road I stuck out my thumb and was immediately picked up in a campavan that took me to the highway where, again immediately, a small yellow pick-up stopped. The driver took me all the way to Banff at great and terrifying speeds, cursing the standard of the rutted all-weather gravel road as he hammered down the middle of it in a cloud of dust.

In Banff, the busiest holiday town in the Rockies, I tramped around for hours looking for accommodation. Everywhere was full, the reason being, I discovered, that a rodeo event called the Calgary Stampede was on in Calgary and overspill visitors were staying in Banff. Eventually I managed to book the last room in the Banff Caribou Lodge. The price of $78 reflected the scarcity of rooms. It was twice what I'd paid elsewhere. I was only intending to stay two nights though. Or so I thought.

Interlude One: Banff Days

July 10th to July 13th

The town of Banff started life as a branch of the Canadian Pacific Railway called, mundanely, Siding 29. The railway arrived in 1883 and the townsite was laid out three years later. The park was established in 1885, initially to preserve some hot springs. Seeing an opportunity to attract customers it was the CPR under the American Cornelius Van Horne which encouraged the growth and development of the resort that is now Banff townsite, building grandiose hotels like the Banff Springs, with its all-Scottish interior design and castle-like exterior, to house its guests. It was Van Horne who named the park after Banffshire in Scotland where the CPR president George Stephen was born. Today Banff National Park, the third to be established in the world, is, at 2500 square miles, second only to Jasper National Park to the north in size among the mountain parks of the Rockies. The townsite itself is the busiest tourist destination in the Rockies.

The day after I arrived was a Sunday which meant an enforced day off. For want of anything better to do, I headed down the crowded high street. Banff was packed with tourists wandering up and down and picking through the titbits in the multitude of gift shops. They looked as though they were trying to convince themselves that they really were having a good time despite the noise and the dust and the traffic and the mosquitos and the lack of anything particularly interesting to do. Back home I could imagine them telling friends how pretty it was, sure, now they weren't there any more, that actually it had been quite nice. A desperate way of killing time I thought. I knew I wasn't enjoying myself. But then, I didn't expect to. This was just a necessary hiatus in the walk. Actually, as I was to discover over the next few days, Banff does have an interesting mountain art gallery, some rather overdeveloped hot springs and a very good bookshop, the Banff Book and Art Den, where I spent several enjoyable hours browsing before purchasing some extra reading matter. There are plenty of pleasant short walks around the town too but I wanted to rest my battered feet and not walk far on what was, after all, a day off from the trek.

One reason for my foot problems was that the running shoes I'd brought with me for campwear and road walking were too tight-fitting, the result of a foolish money-saving ploy which was to cost me dear. They'd been bought in a sale. The only pair I could find in Banff that fitted my wide feet were predictably expensive, $90 in fact. I had no choice but to buy them. I also purchased some Second Skin for my blisters and three pairs of thin wool/cotton socks as my thick ones, designed for British summers, were proving too hot.

As soon as the post office opened Monday morning I was in there asking for my mail, as I wanted to leave by lunchtime. The supply box was there along with some letters from home, the first I'd received. But there was no pack. I went and had a second breakfast and read my mail then came back when they'd sorted the day's deliveries. Still no pack. I decided to wait a day. Tuesday morning came but no pack with it. I phoned England. John was away but his wife Maggie told me the pack had been sent the previous Monday on a guaranteed three-day delivery at a cost of £91. That had been eight days ago. Baffled and frustrated I returned to the post office. Here I was handed a note saying that a courier service in Calgary had phoned to say they had it, but couldn't deliver it as there was no address except the post office, which would not accept privately-mailed parcels. With the feeling that the situation was becoming far too complicated and not a little out of hand, I phoned the couriers. Yes, they had the pack but it was in customs in bond and they couldn't get it out without my permission. If I gave it they might be able to arrange for an attorney to retrieve it. I had to ring back to check. Two phone calls later and I'd established that the courier company did not have customs rights at Calgary but only at Toronto so I would have to go and get the pack myself. By this time it was too late to do so that day so I retreated grimly to a bar cursing private courier companies and their expensive 'guarantees'.

Four nights in the motel being more than I could afford, I packed up and moved out to the Tunnel Mountain Campground a few miles from town. It was $7 a night and a much nicer place to stay. I was sitting staring into my campfire, much cheaper and more entertaining than staring into a glass of beer, when a cyclist rode up. Could he share my site, he asked, and pay half the fee? As the sites were designed for giant campavans with a couple of scout troop tents on the side, I had plenty of room and welcomed him in. Carl looked as though he'd been on the road a long time and so it turned out, for he was on the return journey of a trip from California to Jasper and had been cycling since early April.

My fourth day in Banff brought action at last. I caught a bus to Calgary airport, which I hadn't expected to see again so soon, picked up the new pack, caught a bus back and mailed my old pack home. I phoned John to tell him I had the pack and would soon be on the move again. I was very fed up by this stage but John raised my spirits somewhat by pointing out, quite correctly, that a four-day rest would be very good for my feet and that the break would do me no harm. I could tell he'd once been a social worker! The episode had all been very frustrating but at least I had my new pack and could move on the next day. I was very relieved as I felt that I had more than exhausted all that Banff had to offer.

I had much to look forward to as well, since except for a meagre twenty or so miles, the next 525 miles were all in the mountain parks, a virtual guarantee of superb scenery, good trails and fine campsites. And beyond the parks? The unknown, unwalked almost trailless northern Rockies. But I didn't want to think about them yet. Vacating Banff was my main aim in life now I had a new pack.

Summer in the Mountain Parks

Spray Lakes to Saskatchewan Crossing
14th July to 27th July   185 miles

Heavy rain at dawn did not delay my departure from Banff on the 8.40am bus. I was so desperate to continue the walk that on alighting at the little town of Canmore, where the cross-country skiing events were held in the 1988 Winter Olympics, I caught a taxi, at a cost of $40, to the Mount Shark Trailhead from where I had hitchhiked into Banff five long days before. I was heading for Mount Assiniboine, one of the most impressive peaks in the Rockies. Often called 'the Matterhorn of the Rockies', this 11,870-foot-high spire of rock and snow had caught my imagination when I had seen photographs of it a few years earlier and visiting the peak had been one of my personal goals on the ski tour of 1987, though that visit had only whetted my appetite to spend more time in this spectacular area which I was looking forward to seeing without its covering of snow.

The trail to Lake Magog at the base of the mountain took me past Marvel Lake and over Wonder Pass, the names showing the feelings the area engendered in the first European explorers. The weather slowly improved during the day and as superb views opened out on the steep climb above Marvel Lake the last clouds vanished. Only one tent was on the camp site but there were several people around the private Assiniboine Lodge at the foot of the lake and smoke coming out of the chimneys of every one of the Naiset Cabins where I'd stayed the year before. As I set up camp on the shelf on the far side of the lake from Mount Assiniboine where the campground is situated the magic light of evening swept over the scene. I grabbed my tripod and camera and took many pictures as the waves of darkening light emphasised different aspects of the peak. Nearby, three elk and a calf grazed peacefully. The new pack had felt comfortable despite my heaviest load yet and my feet felt better. The walk was under way again and I felt as though this time I had everything under control.

The other campers were two teenage girls and their father. As I sat watching the evening light I was astonished to see them wander down to the creek and wash their dirty dishes in it and then shampoo their hair in the same place, right under a sign saying 'Drinking Water—no washing anything within 30 metres'. They repeated the performance the next morning. I debated whether to say anything or not. What stopped me was the fact that I was not Canadian and I knew from speaking to them earlier that they were from Edmonton. As locals they might have objected to a foreigner telling them what to do. Later I realised, as several people I mentioned the incident to pointed out, that I really should have remonstrated with them. The fact that I wasn't a local was no more than a convenient excuse for doing nothing.

Taking photographs of Assiniboine in the colder dawn light, a long cloud plume streaming out from the top, I found the warning lights blinking in one of my cameras. The batteries were fading. I changed them only to find the battery lid jamming when I replaced it and the new batteries failing to work. Several minutes' work with a coin and various blades of my pocket knife only succeeded in virtually destroying the screw top. The camera was completely electric with no manual override. I'd brought it as a spare but was using it as my main one due to the self-timer's breaking on my other camera body. Now I had just one working camera and no self-timer. So much for being in control. I was, though, just one day's walk away from the Sunshine Meadows ski resort whose cable cars would be running. Using these I could return to Banff and try and have the camera fixed.

Hail stones greeted me as I wandered through the strange Valley of the Rocks which looked totally different to when I had skied through it the previous year. Then, there were simply many large white hummocks dotted about. Now these were revealed as a vast number of apparently randomly placed boulders. Four parties of backpackers heading for Assiniboine passed me. Most people come in from Sunshine as there is virtually no climbing involved whilst I had a long climb to 7750-foot Citadel Pass to make. Rich flower meadows glistening in the now falling rain made the ascent less of a chore than it might have been. During a gap in the showers a lone walker descended wearing just white shorts and a white tee-shirt. He paused to greet me and I wished him luck with the weather as more black clouds were rolling in from the west. He grinned, 'Oh, these are just showers, they help cool you down' and was off down the trail. The next 'shower' produced torrential and prolonged rain and a cold wind and I reached the pass wearing full waterproofs. I was more than cool enough. Camp that night was not far away at Howard Douglas Lake, an hour or so's walk from the cable car station. At 7500 feet it was the highest camp site of the walk. Because it is so accessible the site is very popular, though I had it to myself that first night. The cold storm blew on and I wore gloves at dinner and was soon ensconced in the tent.

The storm raged all night bringing rain and hail, but at dawn the sky was clear and the tent frozen solid with an outer coating of frost. A brief stroll in the early morning sun with superb views back to distant Mount Assiniboine brought me to the cable car station where the attendant allowed me to have a free ride down with two members of staff, who entertained me by trying to throw empty bottles out of the car and into trash cans when we momentarily halted at intermediate stops. I gathered this was a boredom alleviating game played by those who had to clean out the cabin cars. At the bottom station I was told there were no buses to Banff so reluctantly I ordered a taxi. A bus promptly pulled up. I took it. En route we passed a taxi heading up the steep road. Back in Banff, which I'd sincerely hoped not to see again for a long time, I had a brief wrestle with my conscience. I don't like feeling guilty, so once the feeling had occurred I knew that I would have to pay the taxi company to dispel it. Clearing my conscience cost me $30. The bus had been $5.

In the first camera shop I tried, the assistant couldn't remove the battery holder lid. He suggested it might be a factory job but that I might try a jeweller's: 'They're used to that sort of thing, with watches and so on,' was his reasoning. I went to another camera shop. It took the woman in Arcade Cameras no more than a few minutes to remove the lid, test the batteries, pronounce them dead and replace them, all for a cost of just $8. With time to spare before the bus back to Sunshine I also bought some new insoles for my boots as I suspected that the original ones were the cause of my blisters.

I was back at camp before dark to find three women had joined me. Youth hostel workers who backpacked nearly every weekend, they had heard Ben Gadd lecture and been impressed by him. They clearly weren't as impressed by me as they didn't think I had much chance of completing my walk. Given everything that had gone wrong so far, from my feet to my cameras, I wasn't sure they weren't right. Just as it grew dark two others arrived, making this the most crowded backcountry site I'd used. They were heading for Assiniboine whilst the women were staying here two nights, using it as a base for day walks.

Walking to Sunshine from the lake with the full pack attracted much attention whereas the day before with no pack hardly anyone had even said hello. Now, all the day hikers wanted to know where I was going with such a massive load, which made for slow progress and a dawdling day, not helped by my being unable to resist the temptation of a luxury lunch in the Sunshine Inn. The scenery, though, as I crossed Simpson and Healy Passes was superb and many of the people were very interesting to talk to, including one couple from California who'd just returned from China where they'd climbed a sacred mountain by endless cut granite steps. For more prosaic reasons the heavily-used paths around the ski resort were carefully manicured too. The laid gravel walkways with neat rock edging would have looked more in place in a city park than up here at timberline but I could see why it was necessary; there were people everywhere, far more than I saw anywhere else in the mountains.

Dropping down to Egypt Lake I found the campground there overcrowded. Every official site was full and plenty of tents were pitched where they shouldn't have been. I found the place, situated in a shallow, forested ravine away from the lake with no views, and obviously overused, quite unappealing. As it was 7pm I considered joining the throng anyway but decided I'd rather press on to the next, hopefully less crowded, site over five miles further on. This meant walking hard and fast up a steep 1000-foot climb to the narrow, rocky defile of Whistling Valley, bleak and grey in the dusk with dark peaks looming up all around, where I stopped to take some photographs. A cold wind was whipping through the valley and I assumed such winds had given the place its name, but the Trail Guide told me that it comes from the high-pitched warning cries of the hoary marmots that inhabit its boulder fields. Many of these large, bulky rodents watched and whistled at me as I hurried on through the darkening pass. A quick descent past Haiduk Lake took me down to the Ball Pass Junction campground (so called because it lies at the junction of two trails) which I reached at 9.30pm. I was surprised to find the place deserted, especially as the timberline site, surrounded by the peaks of the Ball Range, was in a spectacular situation. It was, I realised, the first night I'd camped alone since crossing Palliser Pass nine days previously and I relished sitting outside the tent watching the rugged mountain skyline fade into the blackness of night. My only companions were a number of raiding porcupines that had me hanging my pack up to prevent them gnawing it.

Ball Pass Junction, whose morning beauty had me spending an hour on photography before I left, was one of my favourite national park backcountry sites. However that evening I found an even more impressive one and the start of a wonderful three-day walk that must rank as one of the best short backpacking trips in the world. During the day I'd crossed 7800-foot Ball Pass with splendid views of 10,950-foot Mount Ball with its hanging glaciers and then endured a fast, foot-pounding 2900-foot descent to the Banff-Radium Highway. Keeping me going was the view ahead to huge cliffs along the Great Divide, the cliffs of the eastern face of the Vermilion Range known as The Rockwall. Once across the almost empty highway I left Banff for Kootenay National Park and a three-hour, 2300-foot climb through dense forest to Floe Lake, one of the most beautiful alpine lakes I saw on the whole walk. This long timberline lake is backed by the towering 3300-foot high Rockwall itself with miniature glaciers dotted along its foot. The small icebergs that calve off these glacial remnants give the lake its name.

Being so close to a highway Floe Lake is very popular and I'd met three parties descending and then found several tents pitched at the lakeside campground. Although in the backcountry, this is a real campground with gravel tent pads, laid gravel paths, outhouses, picnic tables and even a map showing where the tent pads were. This formality is part of an attempt to minimise the impact from campers and allow previously damaged areas to recover. Whilst it did detract from the wilderness feel of the area I could see the reason for it. My only real objection was to the gravel pads as my tent pegs would not grip properly in the loose surface. Other campers, I noticed, were using large plastic pegs. My site, numbered 12-P, was back in the woods but my eating place overlooked the lake. Most of the evening though was spent down on the lakeshore watching and photographing the beautiful constantly changing reflections of The Rockwall in the smooth waters.

The Rockwall itself runs unbroken by any pass for twenty-five miles along the Great Divide. For nearly twenty of those miles The Rockwall Trail follows the great cliff, a rollercoaster of a route that crosses three alpine passes with sharp drops into the intervening valleys and similarly rapid, if steep, climbs back out. Any feelings of weariness caused by the strenuous effort required to walk this trail are totally wiped away by the sheer intensity of the mountain beauty that unfolds as the hours go by. A succession of hanging glaciers, high peaks, tumbling waterfalls, clear rushing streams, flower meadows and tree groves leads the walker effortlessly on. I spent a day and a half on the trail and wished I could have stayed for many more. After photographing a delicate, pastel pink sunrise along the length of Floe Lake that touched the grey limestone of the cliffs with momentary colour, I left the lake and climbed 1000 feet in a mile and a half to the highest point on the trail—7800-foot Numa Pass—dropped instantly 2700 feet down to forested Numa Creek, then went straight back up 2250 feet to Tumbling Pass. Both the passes gave extensive views along The Rockwall with the sharp pyramid of 10,550-foot Foster Peak dominant. On Tumbling Pass I met two wardens on horseback. 'Do you have a permit?' they asked. 'Yes,' I replied, feeling somewhat guilty and hoping they wouldn't ask to see it as my permit had been altered several times and was anyway out of date.

A descent by a loose, gravelly terminal moraine led to Tumbling Creek campground, another fine site on the edge of some meadows with The Rockwall soaring above. I'd only walked eleven miles but the next site was over six miles and two more stiff ascents away so I stopped. In this sort of terrain how far you go each day depends as much on the amount of climbing to be done as on mileage. I had the site to myself though it was clearly well-used with bare patches of hard-packed earth all around. A network of wooden stakes marking out tent pads and cooking areas suggested that it was to be improved in the way the Floe Lake campground had been. This would be a pity, I thought, as despite the well-used appearance this site had a wilderness feel that had gone from Floe Lake.

Far above the campground the last rays of the sun picked out the upper reaches of the well-named Tumbling Glacier which looked as though it was defying gravity in remaining suspended high on the cliffs. Later a crescent moon curved into the sky above the glacier and had me reaching for my camera and tripod. As there was much precut wood stacked up I lit a small fire in a dusty firepit beside which a new stake was stuck in the ground with the word 'firepit' clearly inscribed on it.

During the night a porcupine attempted to make off with my boots and I had to bring them in the tent to keep them safe. I also hung the pack up and whilst doing so thanked the porcupine for forcing me out of the tent, for a magnificent starry sky lay above the black silhouette of the jagged Rockwall. At 6am I glanced out of the tent door, left open as there were no mosquitos, to see bright sunlight on the cliffs contrasting with the dark shadowed forest in the foreground. Reluctant though I was to leave my warm sleeping bag for the chilly dawn air I knew I had to take some photographs. There was anyway a long sixteen-mile day with much climbing ahead so I needed an early start. Since leaving Sunshine the weather had grown hotter and hotter and on this day I recorded a temperature of 45°C in the sun at midday!

A swift ascent to the spreading meadows of the Wolverine Plateau led, in the words of my journal, to 'perhaps the best scenery yet' along a magnificent section of trail between Rockwall Pass and Limestone Summit. The Rockwall is cleft briefly here by the narrow square cut gash of 7200-foot Wolverine Pass between Mount Grey and Mount Drysdale, both 9500 feet high, which is only seen when the walker is directly opposite it. A pleasant bonus was the sight of a herd of mountain goats browsing casually along the ledges of a steep crag. Three female backpackers ascending with loads at least as big as mine gasped out a greeting as I began the descent to Helmet Creek and the finish of the Rockwall Trail. As I dropped down through the trees on a steep trail, the roaring of water grew louder and louder until I came to an avalanche chute opening and could see at the head of the valley the mighty 1200-foot drop of Helmet Falls crashing down from a vast rock amphitheatre. The path led down almost to the base of this great waterfall and then away down the valley to a 1500-foot climb in two and a half miles to Goodsir Pass on the boundary between Kootenay and Yoho National Parks. High above the flower-filled pass soared the 11,860-foot twin peaks of Mount Goodsir. To the south I had my last views of the Rockwall fading away into the distance. A warden on horseback passed me heading for Helmet Falls, pausing to warn me there were fresh grizzly diggings in the meadows here and also that a change in the weather was forecast. High cirrus clouds away to the west had already made me wonder about whether a storm was approaching.

Dehydration is usually only a problem on long ascents, especially above timberline, so I was not expecting to feel thirsty on the wooded descent to the Ottertail River and didn't bother to refill my water bottle at the pass. But the long steep, dusty and waterless trail through dense heat-trapping forest had me gasping for water and plunging my head into the cold stream at the bottom. This unpleasant and tiring descent was mitigated only by views across Goodsir Creek below me to the vast north-east face of Mount Goodsir, rising an incredible 6400-feet from the creek bed to the summit. Beyond the bridged Ottertail River I came to a warden cabin with a trail crew sunbathing and drinking beer outside. They looked irritatingly cool and relaxed to me as I stumbled past, hot, weary and sticky with sweat, to pitch the tent in McArthur Campground, set in dense lodgepole pine forest. Again I was alone, though a disappointingly large amount of garbage showed the site had been used recently. I burnt all I could then wandered down to the riverbank to sit and watch Mount Goodsir fade into the night. At 9.15pm the temperature was still 25°C. A constant succession of single high-pitched notes that could have been made by a bird or a small mammal started as soon as I tried to go to sleep. I slipped out of the tent, naked in the warm night, with just a head lamp and padded over the soft pine needles towards a source of the noise. Seeing a small dark object on a branch about ten feet off the ground I shone my lamp on it. An owl blinked and stared back. Back in the tent I identified it from *The Handbook* as a northern pygmy owl. 'Gives forth cute little hoots, but over and over, monotonously,' wrote Ben Gadd. Monotonous certainly. Cute I wasn't so sure about as several of the owls called for hours, keeping me awake.

'A rich habitat for many large mammals, including grizzly bear. Stay alert while hiking this valley,' warned the Trail Guide of the trail up McArthur Creek to McArthur Pass. During the six-mile, 2400-foot climb I found fresh bear droppings on the trail. With no signs or warnings I hadn't given bears much thought in recent days but suddenly I found myself anxiously surveying the avalanche slopes I was crossing for any

47

movement. Near the pass a warden, on foot for once, greeted me. The first thing Alan Knowles the Lake O'Hara warden, as I later discovered he was, mentioned was the bear sign. Had I seen any grizzlies? Then he really startled me. 'You're not called Townsend, are you?' he asked. Shirley Green of the Yoho Park Warden Service to whom I'd sent a supply box had become worried about me as I was nine days late and had put a call out, asking wardens to look out for me. She'd traced me as far as Elkford but no further. I hadn't let her know I would be late as I'd revised my permit dates in Banff all the way to Field and I'd assumed this information would be passed on. In fact when Shirley had asked the Banff park office if I'd been through they'd said no. The warden said he'd radio through to say I'd been located and would arrive soon.

Shortly beyond the pass I reached Lake O'Hara, a very popular destination with a campground and both commercial and Alpine Club of Canada cabins and lodges. Part of the popularity is due to there being a bus service up the forest road to the lake (closed to cars) but the main reason is the classic alpine scenery that surrounds the lake and the extensive and intricate trail network that makes the area a good base for day walks. Dominating the view are Mounts Lefroy (11,230-feet) and Victoria (11,350-feet) though there are many more high peaks in the area. A notice in the warden cabin window dated July 7–13 warned that three grizzlies were active in the McArthur Creek drainage. I had a snack of Coca-Cola and chocolate in the rather grand Lake O'Hara Lodge before taking a long, winding but scenic trail down to the Trans-Canada Highway. Ahead of me across the highway were the high pass and steep slopes down which Todd and I had descended after the ten-day Wapta Icefields traverse we had made fourteen months earlier. They looked both familiar and strange without their coating of snow. Down at the noisy, busy highway I had a meal in the West Louise Lodge where Todd and I had celebrated the end of our ski tour. I hardly imagined then that I would be back again only just over a year later.

Five best-forgotten miles led down the road to the crowded Kicking Horse Campground. The main site being full, I camped on the crowded overspill site amongst ragged trees and sandy soil on the floodplain of the Kicking Horse River. All was dry and dusty but I wondered what happened when it rained. Later in the summer I was to read of a near-disaster here when a heavy storm caused a mudslide that overwhelmed the campground turning over campavans and flooding the valley as well as sweeping over the railway and highway. Although much damage was caused, thankfully no-one was hurt. I was too tired to care about the decline in campsite standards having walked 21 miles in under 10 hours, including two hour-long stops on another very hot day. The tiny café-cum-store provided me with Coca-Cola and two tins of mandarin oranges, one for supper, one for breakfast. I was out of food but only a short walk from Field and my next supply box.

My tiredness meant I slept well despite the incredible rumble of the trains on the nearby railroad and the lesser noise of trucks on the highway. Over breakfast I worked out a schedule for the next eight days and then obtained the necessary permits from the park office in the campground before walking the 2$^{1}/_{2}$ miles of highway to the little railway town of Field. Here I collected my third supply box from Shirley Green at the park headquarters, then checked into Amwiski Hostel which she owns. After a nice veggie pittabread lunch in a tiny café called The Sidings I encountered an unforeseen difficulty. Field had no bank and I had no cash. The hardly bearable possibility of having to return to Banff loomed ominously up before I realised with relief that Lake Louise was nearer, just a short bus ride away in fact. However, the town itself offered no facilities for obtaining cash short of robbery, the bank not taking either Visa or Access, so I took another bus up to the grand Chateau Lake Louise hotel where Todd and I had enjoyed luxurious accommodation on our ski trip courtesy of the head chef Jari Nydr whom we'd met and skied with in the Mount Assiniboine area. Unfortunately I had no time to look Jari up but had to rush back to the town to catch the train to Field once I had cashed some money at the hotel. The latter descends from Kicking Horse Pass via a complex system of spiral tunnels to alleviate the grade which makes for an interesting journey.

Back at the hostel quite an international party had assembled, as seems the norm for hostels these days, including a combined German-Israeli-Australian party who had met at another hostel. They were trying out all the Rockies had to offer and had so far been river rafting, horse riding and hiking. A French couple had a more relaxed approach and were touring Canada by car. Shirley introduced me to later arrivals Don Beers and his wife; Don was a writer and author of the local guidebook *The Magic of Lake O'Hara*. He felt, not surprisingly, that it was a pity I wasn't spending more time in the area. We discussed the next section of my route and he told me that he was not impressed with the Iceline Trail, only opened that summer and which I was to follow, as there was too much moraine to cross and that he much preferred the lower Highline Trail which it replaced. Shirley also gave me some route advice especially regarding a section in a little-visited part of Yoho Park and the following few miles that were not in the park at all. My problem was that staying close to the Great Divide, as I had done so far, was no longer possible due to the almost unbroken chain of icefields that lace the main crest of the Rockies from here north to Yellowhead Pass. It was some of these icefields that I'd skied over the previous year. I knew from that trip that there is no route for backpackers through this area of permanent snow and ice. My plan was firstly to head west of the icefields before cutting through them via Howse Pass, an easy ice-free crossing, and then follow the Front Ranges to Jasper before heading west again around the north end of the ice. The Front Ranges are so-named because they are the first range of mountains west of the great plains. They are almost as high as the Main Ranges but being in the latter's rain shadow they don't have the same amount of snowfall or as big glaciers.

Shirley treated me to breakfast the next morning before I shouldered my now full-again pack and headed out of Field for the 4-mile 3000-foot climb to Burgess Pass. Below me the little town dwindled to doll's house size. Beyond the pass the trail contoured across the open slopes of Mount Field and Wapta Mountain below the World Heritage Site of the Burgess Shale Beds. Here and on Mount Stephen across the Kicking Horse valley in 1909, palaeontologist Sir Charles Walcott discovered a rich bed of complete soft-bodied Cambrian fossils, a unique find. The beds are now strictly protected and a special permit is needed to visit them. I'd been told in Field that a part of scientists was working there over the summer and as I passed below the area I could see high up on the mountainside the tents of their camp. My eye was drawn also to the bright waters of Emerald Lake glistening in the forest far below and to the north the peaks of the Presidential Range. I met many day hikers on the descent to Yoho Pass and Yoho Lake and the start of the Highline Trail. As I left the trees I was treated to stupendous views of the Yoho Valley and its surrounding peaks and glaciers and, tumbling in a 1247-foot rainbow-speckled arc from the Daly Glacier, the Rockies' highest waterfall, Takakkaw Falls, the thunder of its roaring descent echoing all around.

A high-level route along the western slopes of the Yoho Valley was first made by a party led by Edward Whymper in 1901. He was here as a guest of the CPR and they built the Highline Trail at his suggestion. So popular has it been since, that the park authorities are considering closing it to allow the meadows along its route to recover from the heavy use. As a replacement they have built an even higher route, the Iceline Trail, that runs over the moraines below the long snout of the Emerald Glacier. This is the route that Don Beers disliked, as did a party of four backpackers I passed who complained about the hard underfoot surface and the constant ups and downs. They also admitted that they weren't happy this far above the forest. My view was the complete opposite. I thought it a marvellous trail as it wound around the glacial melt pools below the deeply crevassed glacier wall over miles of moraine and outwashes with, to the north and east, the Waputik Icefield, which I'd skied over the previous year, with its rock peaks rising dark above the white snowfields. I stopped to take many photographs and to absorb the views and high mountain atmosphere, so it was late in the evening when I strolled into the Little Yoho Campground which was crowded with tents and people. The numbers weren't surprising as the site is only just over three miles from the roadhead at Takakkaw Falls and is ideally positioned for both day walks and alpine climbs in the surrounding mountains. There is also an Alpine Club of Canada hut here, the Stanley Mitchell Hut, and indeed many of the people I spoke to were climbers rather than walkers. One climber, who'd been up the peak called The President that day and who looked to be in his late fifties himself, on hearing of my planned off-trail route, told me that an 'elderly' hiker travelling very light with no stove and no tent had gone the same way that day.

I left the trail network at 8038-foot Kiwetinok Pass, a rocky slash in the mountains that gave excellent views of ranges of snowy peaks disappearing into the west. Below, the Kiwetinok Valley curved away to the south-west, down to the Amwiski River and its adjacent fire road. I needed to reach the latter but preferably further to the north. I consulted the *Trail Guide*. 'No trail exists . . . by contouring over the northwest ridge of Kiwetinok Valley it is possible to eventually reach the abandoned logging roads leading down to Amwiski.' A careful perusal of the north-west ridge showed a col that might provide a way down on the other side. Between the pass and the ridge swept a steep scree-covered mountainside with some larger boulderfields, rocky spurs and small wind-stunted trees or krumholz on the far side.

The traverse to the ridge required great care as I scrambled over outcrops of rock and slithered across the loose scree above small cliffs, glad that my new pack was proving very stable and also that I had my walking stick for extra support. This was not a place to slip. Most difficult though was the final climb to the col through a giant, springy mattress of dense krumholz. Every few feet gained required an amazing amount of effort and I was exhausted when I reached the windswept col. As I sat down for a rest an elk stag appeared from the other side, halted in surprise, then ran back the way it had come. Where an elk could ascend I was sure I could descend. In fact the going proved easier than on the traverse from Kiwetinok Pass at first as I raced down easy-angled scree and snow slopes. My progress was halted abruptly, though, when I reached timberline. A graveyard of dead trees spread as far as I could see, the results of what must have been a major forest fire. There was no sign of any logging roads nor did I find any as I descended laboriously through the tangled mass of fallen burnt timber and dense undergrowth. On reaching the Amwiski River I found that the whole of that valley was burnt too, which explained

51

why the park authorities allowed backpackers to camp where they liked. I can't imagine many people choose to come here.

The realities of cross-country travel sank in as I worked out that I had only travelled five and a half miles in six and a quarter hours. The implications for the second half of the walk which would be mostly cross-country were too worrying to think about so I shoved them firmly to the back of my mind to be considered seriously only when they had to be. For the moment though my problems were over as I had the old fire road to follow up the devastated valley past Amwiski Falls, a delicate tracery of water that brought a little brightness into the stark black and grey of the burnt trees that pointed lifelessly into the sky. As I neared Amiskwi Pass the fire road gave way to a sketchy trail and green trees began to appear. Shirley Green, who had a cabin high above the pass, had suggested traversing across the slopes above timberline for a way before dropping down to the Blaeberry River from the pass and the *Trail Guide* said that: 'from Amwiski Pass to the Blaeberry River a thick bushwhack to the Collie Creek logging road can be shortened by keeping above timberline until the last possible moment'.

Given the above I was surprised to find an excellent trail leading down from the pass into the Ensign Creek valley especially as I was no longer on national park land. As it could hardly go anywhere but in the right direction I followed it. Soon I came to the first of a series of new clear-cut areas on the edge of which I set up a rather uncomfortable camp. I'd ended up walking 12 miles but it had taken me ten hours. I was too tired to reflect on this though, which was probably just as well.

Clouds of mosquitos greeted me at dawn, so I had an early start on what I was to describe in my journal as a 'frustrating, confusing day'. It began straightforwardly enough as I followed the trail beside Ensign Creek until it ran into a network of logging roads which I kept to as they traversed above the valley, giving good views of the rugged, glacier-covered peaks of the Mummery Group to the west. When the road turned south-west and began to descend I decided to bushwhack straight down to the Blaeberry River and save myself some distance. The slope was very steep and heavily vegetated and it took me an hour to slip and slide down it, encountering en route the thick feather-moss typical of such shaded places. Unfortunately this dense mat is both loose and deep and makes for difficult progress. I reached the fast and wide glacier-grey river at a point where the banks rose steeply to the south but levelled out to the north in which direction I was able to follow the river to another logging road and a bridge over it that I needed to cross. At a distance the bridge looked fine. However as I approached, I began to realise that most of it had been swept away and that the few massive struts still reaching out across the churning water did not reach the other side. I didn't need to leave the bank to realise that this river was unfordable on foot. A little further on, Collie Creek, another foaming torrent, joined the main river and I was caught between the two. The bridge over the Collie looked slightly more promising as one of the main beams, although washed by the waves, still touched both banks. On my side it rested on a large boulder. Discarding the pack I gingerly crawled onto it from the top of the boulder. Immediately it began to slowly twist over. I edged a few inches out from the boulder on the wet, slippery wood. The log rolled sideways with each move. I looked down into the fast, grey, white-waved water sliding past a few feet below me. Once in that with a pack on I'd have no chance. I crawled backwards to the safety of the boulder and considered my position. I had to cross one of these rivers. I knew I could not follow the Blaeberry downstream because of the cliffs I'd seen so I took the only option which was to follow the Collie upstream.

I'd only gone a short distance though when I noticed some coloured flagging dangling from a bush. Beyond it a trail started to climb steeply up the hillside. I consulted my map. Above me lay the logging road which would take me down to another bridge if I could regain it. As the road looked recently used I guessed this bridge would still be in place. The trail was new and well-maintained and led up for a thousand feet to the logging road just before the point where I'd bushwhacked down to the river. More flagging marked where the trail left the road, flagging I'd missed previously. It seemed odd that a new trail should lead down into a cul-de-sac. I stuck to the road even though it headed south. I was sunk in a circular series of rather depressed thoughts about the lack of progress I was making when something on the road about twenty yards ahead caught my attention. A small black bear, the first bear of the walk, was crossing the road. As I paused so did the bear, turning to look in my direction, before bolting away through the trees. A roar and cloud of dust behind me produced the first of three pick-ups. Their presence told me the bridge must be intact. Two of them stopped to offer rides.

Once across the very solid bridge I followed the road up beside the Blaeberry to the washed-out bridge to complete an unnecessary six-mile loop. If only, I thought, I hadn't decided to bushwhack straight down to the river. Beware short cuts! The road continued up the valley well beyond where it was marked as ending on the map to a recreation site clearly well-used by horse parties. I used it too as the dense, mossy forest didn't look ideal terrain for finding an unprepared site. Picnic tables, fire rings and an outhouse made for an unexpectedly comfortable camp. Also unexpected and even more welcome was the sign across the road from the site marking the start of the 'Howse Pass Trail'. Once I reached the pass I would re-enter Banff National Park. With a trail there it looked as though my difficulties were over.

A porcupine snuffling around outside woke me at midnight just in time to see a huge moon rising down the valley which had me leaping naked out of the tent to take some pictures. I didn't notice any cold at the time but the dawn came with a –2°C temperature. My optimism of the evening before lasted just two and a half hours, the time it took me to walk the first five miles of the trail. This brought me to an unnamed, unbridged creek that tore down over a grinding bouldery bed into the Blaeberry. I stared at the silt-filled water as it rushed past. If it wasn't too deep I might be able to ford it. The distance was only about twenty-five feet. I ventured into the creek, holding onto a bush that grew out over the water. My feet were nearly swept from under me as I went in over my knees only a couple of feet out from the bank. I hastily scrambled back onto dry land. I was trapped on a small spit of land between this creek and the river for only a couple of dozen yards upstream the creek came tumbling down a series of waterfalls in a deep chasm. High above these cascades I could see the ice of the Lambe Glacier which fed the creek. After weeks of hot weather the summer glacier melt was at its height.

In case there was a way across I fought my way up the densely vegetated and steep slopes beside the creek, but only found myself perched on the edge of the cliff-rimmed gorge. I spent most of the afternoon prospecting back along the banks of the Blaeberry searching for a way across but to no avail. Returning to the Lambe Glacier outflow creek and still watching the river in case I'd missed a potential ford, I bumped into something with my head. Turning I saw a hornets' nest hanging down gracefully from the branch of a tree. The inhabitants were already beginning to buzz around angrily so I turned hastily away but not fast enough to prevent one of them stinging me right in the middle of the forehead, the only time I was attacked or injured by an animal on the whole walk.

Back at the confluence of the streams I did the only thing possible and made camp. I then cut notches on a stick which I placed in the creek so that I could monitor the rise and fall of the water. The volume of water in glacial streams falls during the night as the temperature drops and the glaciers cease melting. The lowest water level is usually early in the morning and I hoped I would be able to cross then. I set my watch alarm for 5am. In the meantime I spent the rest of the day washing out my clothes for the first time in two weeks and hanging them out in the hot sun to dry and studying my maps. Clouds drifted in from the west during the evening and gave rise to a brief five minute shower before dissolving into a fantastic rapidly changing skyscape of spirals and whirls lit by the last rays of the setting sun. However, although this show was spectacular it left me worried that the night would be warm and the water level would not drop.

A dull almost overcast dawn with a few red tinges on the clouds was not promising. The creek had only dropped about six inches but the water was clearer and I could now see the bed in places and the outlines of boulders under the water. 'Probably crossable with care,' I wrote in my journal. The first attempt nearly had me swept off my feet and into the Blaeberry. A second try a few yards upstream had me clinging terrified to my quivering walking stick in deep, strong and cold crutch-deep water but I made it across safely. I was shaking as I scrambled out of the water with a mixture of relief and fear. It had been a risky ford and left me more scared of the river crossings I knew I would have to do to finish the walk than of anything else—including grizzly bears.

A brisk march up the trail soon had me dry, warm and calm again. Howse Pass was still and silent, the surrounding hills capped with cloud. The pass is important in the history of the fur trade and a large painted wooden information sign has been erected which reads: 'First major trade expedition west of the Rockies and led by 'mapmaker' David Thompson descended this pass on June 25 1807 en route to Columbia & Kootenay Rivers'. Thompson was an Englishman working for the North West Company and was guided by local Kootenay Indians whom he recruited as trappers. An accomplished surveyor and map-maker, Thompson was a key figure in the exploration of the Canadian Rockies. He was sent out to find routes to the west in order that the Americans wouldn't dominate the Pacific coast after the successful Lewis and Clark expedition to the south in 1804–5.

Drizzle started falling as I began my descent alongside the Howse River into Banff park having now crossed the Great Divide. At the first creek I came to I found two backpackers camped round a smouldering fire. They were out here for the fishing and had forded the Howse the day before, for which they'd used and needed a rope. The trail itself, they told me, was underwater further downstream. The high waters had meant they'd not had much luck with the fishing though they seemed happy enough— perhaps due to the rum they were drinking, a liberal shot of which helped me on my way down the trail. The writers of the *Trail Guide* weren't impressed with this route at all. 'The way is rough and rooty and depressing,' they said. I was just glad to be making progress again after the frustrations of the previous two days. After a long section in thick forest I came out onto broad river flats where the trail did indeed disappear into a flooded area. When I found myself nearly waist deep in the murky water I paddled out to the bank and bushwhacked along the forest edge for a few hundred yards until the trail returned to the trees. Rounding a corner I saw a figure in blue jeans, a khaki shirt and a bright yellow baseball cap sitting on a tree stump. As I approached he kept calling out loudly but didn't look up from his task of spreading something on a thick slice of bread with a fairly hefty clasp knife. When I was a few feet away I said 'hello' only to see him jump up with shock. His cries were meant to warn off bears but he hadn't heard or seen me approach.

I joined him for lunch and he asked me about the route ahead as he was heading over Howse Pass and then down the Blaeberry valley to the town of Golden, the route of the old fur trappers, as he was interested in the history of the fur trade. He then told me a very complicated family history that involved his surname's changing from Bradley to Keates at some point and perhaps back again so I couldn't work out which he currently was. Either way his first name was Keith and he was a 60-year-old retired school teacher on his first backpacking trip for seventeen years. His external frame pack he said weighed 65 pounds and was too heavy. It was the same one he'd had in 1971 and had only a thin webbing waist strap. I wouldn't have wanted to carry 30lb in it, let alone 65. As we talked he packed up, a laborious process as much of his gear had to be strapped on the outside of the small packbag. Finally he spread a blue down-filled jacket over the back of the pack and lashed it down with what he described as 'my wife's favourite piece of cord, from Spain'. I warned him about the flooded trail ahead and the Lambe Glacier outflow creek crossing which made him curse the park warden he'd consulted for advice as he had been told the walk would be straightforward. He then shouldered his uncomfortable and cumbersome-looking load and headed off towards the pass. I never found out if he completed his walk. I hope so but somehow I doubt it.

Further down the trail I came to the deep, narrow gorge called Mistaya Canyon where the Mistaya River has carved a twisting channel through the rocks. From the bridge over the canyon one can look down into its depths and see the water-smoothed rocks and far below the thin green line of the river. Many people were here as the canyon is only a short stroll from the Icefields Parkway, the main highway between Banff and Jasper townsites and probably one of the few roads in the world where one can gain an impression of what it's like to be in high mountain country as it passes beneath the glaciers and icefields of the Main Ranges. Indeed one glacier, the Athabasca, up which we had started our ski crossing of the Columbia Icefield in 1987, reaches almost to the road. Because of its spectacular situation the parkway is popular with tourists and also with cyclists who come from all over the world to ride its 180 miles. A series of youth hostels caters for the cyclists and also for the ice climbers who come here in winter to ascend the frozen waterfalls of the Weeping Wall which overlooks the highway.

An hour's walk down the road took me to Saskatchewan River

Crossing where there is a motel, café and shop. Rain was falling and I'd walked 23 miles, my second longest day, so I allowed weakness to overcome me and I checked into the motel and ate in the restaurant. Heavy rain the next day kept me there, my diary succinctly describing the day's activities: 'Slept, ate, did laundry, bathed'. I also sent postcards to my supply points informing them that I was running eleven days behind schedule and rang Ben Gadd who was unable to join me on the trails between here and the Jasper townsite as he'd hoped to do, but who invited me to stay with him when I reached the townsite, as I hoped to do in a week.

Along The Glacier and Skyline Trails

Saskatchewan Crossing to Jasper
July 29 to August 7   122 miles
After ten miles on the busy highway I was glad to leave the roar of the
campavans and the smell of petrol for the shade and quiet of the forest
even though the climb out of the valley to Sunset Pass is described in the
Trail Guide as 'excruciating': 2380 feet of ascent is gained in a distance of
two and a half miles, quite steep enough on a hot afternoon. However the
climb was mitigated by a good trail and halfway up I had an excuse for a
rest when I came upon six heavily-laden horses blocking the way. Straining
to pull the ropes tight on one of the loads was a figure dressed in cowboy
hat, checked shirt and blue jeans. The packtrain, he told me, was heading
for the meadows near Sunset Pass where the Brewsters company had a
large summer base camp for walkers and climbers. He was making this
trip, bringing in supplies or clients, nearly every day. The company, whose
buses can be seen on every highway in Banff Park, have run summer
camps in different locations since Bill and Jim Brewster set up an outfitting
service in the park in 1900 though since 1965 it has been owned by the
Greyhound bus company. Although it was large I probably wouldn't even
see the outfitters' camp as it was well-hidden, said the packer, and a sign
had been put up for the park campsite as the outfitters' side trail was much
bigger than the main one due to all the horse traffic. Certainly I noticed
after the horses had disappeared ahead how worn the trail was and how
many new parallel tracks there were.

Three backpackers with large pack frames almost ran into me as they
hurried down the trail but they were not in such a rush that they couldn't
stop and enthuse to me about the campsite I was heading for, where they'd
spent the last four days, and how beautiful the area was. They were quite
right in their praise as I found when the climb finally eased off and I came
out of the forest into vast open meadows with peaks rising all round. At
the campground, situated in a grove of fir trees on the meadow's edge, I

58

found a disappointing amount of rubbish, including a large plastic tarp, which I burnt and which left me wondering how people who were so clearly inspired by this place could leave such a mess. The clean-up and supper over I sat myself on a tree stump looking west over the North Saskatchewan Valley to the massive Main Range summits of Mounts Amery and Saskatchewan. A chilly breeze blew up the valley and the clear sky promised a frost. Far across the meadow I could see the small dots of two anglers by the gleam of a distant pool. An ermine (stoat) danced through the camp in and out of squirrel holes then away down the trail. It was a peaceful evening.

The calm was shattered at 11.30pm when I was woken by the sound of shouting. I looked out of the tent and saw several torches flashing where the trail came out of the forest. I shone my own light to help whomever it was locate the site and about twenty minutes later four shadowy figures loomed up laden with fishing gear. They'd been shouting to warn off bears, having come up the whole trail in the dark. Within a few minutes they'd set up their tents and silence reigned again. When I woke at 7.30am they'd already moved on and their sudden arrival could almost have been a dream. Clouds and pale sunshine made for interesting early morning light on Mount Amery but the clouds of mosquitos rather curtailed my photographic efforts as did the distraction of a number of humming birds that buzzed in and out of the camp like huge bees.

A day of rapidly changing scenery and location followed as I descended steeply out of Banff National Park into the White Goat Wilderness Area, climbed equally steeply up to a high pass and entry into Jasper National Park then down again to camp. Trail maintenance is sketchy in wilderness areas, which are parts of national forests protected from any development including logging, and often only carried out by outfitters and others users. Once I'd crossed the national park boundary at Sunset Pass I found many fallen trees across the trail as I descended in to Cline River valley. There are no bridges either but I managed to cross Huntington and Cataract Creeks via fairly solid log jams and so was able to reassure two backpackers I met descending from Cataract Pass as I began the ascent that they would have no problems. They in turn were able to tell me that there was a rough trail up to the pass. The long wooded climb opened up as I gained height to reveal beautiful flower meadows and a rugged cirque backed by hanging glaciers and rock peaks. There being no restrictions on camping in wilderness areas I began to consider an above-timberline camp in this impressive alpine bowl. However the meadows around the tree line were full of mounds of freshly dug earth, signs that grizzly bears had been digging up ground squirrels to eat. As there was nowhere to hang food a high camp didn't seem advisable with such new bear sign around. Others were prepared to take the risk, though, for five tents were dotted around the cirque. I spoke to the occupant of one who told me he'd come over Cataract Pass from the other direction and that the way was steep but straightforward. He intended staying here a few days and exploring some of the remoter valleys and passes.

Although I'd already walked seventeen miles and it was 5.30pm I decided to head for Boulder Creek Campground in Jasper National Park, seven and a half miles and a steep pass away. Steep scree and extensive snow patches made for a strenuous ascent to 8100-foot Cataract Pass, the highest point I had yet reached. On the pass I admired the fine panorama of peaks but also looked with concern considering the late hour, at the trackless, steep and loose slopes that led down into the valley below. I set off immediately on a straight slithering descent, with diversions round the occasional small cliff, that brought me down to a large moraine lake at the toe of a small and dirty glacier that marks the headwaters of the South Fork of the Brazeau River. My progress slowed down as I made my way along the flat upper valley over a mixture of soft, wet sand and pale red and yellow boulders over which I had to scramble. The terrain was not the only reason for taking my time though. The sun was now low in the sky and a wonderful evening light gave an almost other-worldly feel to this austere yet beautiful valley. The best light was behind me so I was constantly turning round to take photographs and gaze at the darkening landscape. It was 9.15pm when I finally arrived at the small timberline campsite after a 12¹/₂-hour day during which I'd walked 24 miles.

I was now in Jasper National Park, the largest, at 4200 square miles, of the mountain parks. The name comes from the North West Company employee Jasper Hawes who built Jasper House on the Athabasca River in 1812. In 1907 the upper Athabasca River basin was declared a national park, the townsite being founded three years later. The park lies along the eastern side of the Great Divide with Banff National Park to the south, the Willmore Wilderness to the north and the Mount Robson Provincial Park to the north-west. I was to stay in the park for fifteen out of the next twenty-two days, the rest of the time being spent in the Mount Robson park.

Two dome tents were already pitched on the Boulder Creek Campground site and a man was putting up a small orange ridge tent as I arrived. I located the only flattish piece of bare ground left and quickly set up my tent before hanging my food. This was my first camp in Jasper National Park and I was to find the sites different to those in the other mountain parks. To begin with they were more basic with no prepared tent pads, gravel paths or pulley systems for hanging food. Instead of the latter, most sites had a pole nailed between two trees for suspending supplies,

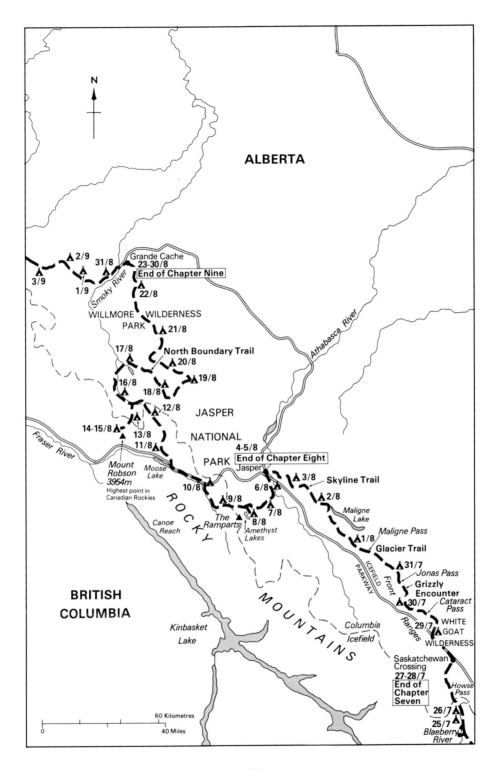

N

ALBERTA

2/9
31/8
3/9
1/9
Smoky River
Grande Cache
23-30/8
End of Chapter Nine
22/8

WILLMORE WILDERNESS
PARK
21/8

17/8
North Boundary Trail
20/8
16/8
19/8
18/8
12/8
JASPER

14-15/8
13/8
11/8
NATIONAL

4-5/8
End of Chapter Eight
PARK
Jasper
3/8 **Skyline Trail**
6/8
2/8

Fraser River

Mount
Robson
3954m
Highest point in
Canadian Rockies
*Moose
Lake*
10/8
9/8
7/8
8/8
*The
Ramparts*
*Amethyst
Lakes*
*Maligne
Lake*
Maligne Pass
1/8 **Glacier Trail**

*Canoe
Reach*

**BRITISH
COLUMBIA**

*Kinbasket
Lake*

R O C K Y

M O U N T A I N S

*Columbia
Icefield*

31/7
Jonas Pass
**Grizzly
Encounter**
*Cataract
Pass*
30/7
29/7 **WHITE
GOAT
WILDERNESS**

ICEFIELD PARKWAY
Front Ranges

Saskatchewan
Crossing
27-28/7
**End of
Chapter
Seven**
*Howse
Pass*

26/7
25/7
*Blaeberry
River*

Athabasca River

60 Kilometres
0
40 Miles

61

campers having to provide their own cord or rope. The Boulder Creek Campground bear pole was located in the middle of the site only a few yards from the tents and I wandered over there to hang my food as soon as I'd pitched the tent. Two men were standing talking under the pole, one of them the owner of the now haphazardly erected orange tent. He was holding a clear plastic bag containing several loaves of bread and staring up at the pole. 'I haven't brought any cord, I thought there'd be cables,' he said, followed by the alarming statement that bears were only interested in meat and as he had just bread and jam he'd leave it on the ground. Knowing that bread was just as likely to attract bears as meat I said he could hang his food with mine as I didn't feel comfortable about spending a night with food on the ground close to the tent even if he did.

The man with no cord, whose name I never found out, was from Calgary but, he said, he shouldn't be here, wherever it was. He should have been with one of the parties camped the other side of Cataract Pass. As he didn't have a map it was quite difficult to work out where he'd come from but eventually it transpired that he'd come up the Nigel Pass Trail from the Icefields Parkway and then turned left instead of right, I listened to this tale in disbelief, my conviction that it was just about impossible to get lost in the mountain parks trail system completely destroyed. I noticed too that the man was wearing smooth-soled, black city shoes, a strange choice I thought for camp shoes. But they weren't camp shoes. 'I forgot my boots,' he announced. The other camper and I exchanged looks. No boots, no map, no cord. What was this person doing here? 'I drove up straight from work,' he continued, 'and when I unloaded the car my boots weren't there.' In my mind his name changed from the man with no cord to the man with no boots. The next day he said he was going to cross Cataract Pass and try and catch up with his party who were doing my route of the last two days in reverse. Wouldn't they wait for him? No, he'd told them if he didn't turn up the first night it meant he'd decided not to come on the trip. I thought of him trying to negotiate the difficult, steep, loose and complex terrain on either side of the pass in city shoes whilst attempting to navigate with no map through an area with only sketchy trails and no signposts and suggested, very gently, that he might be better off heading back the way he had come. I was sure if he went on he'd either slip and have an accident or else get hopelessly lost and wander off into the remote eastern parts of the White Goat Wilderness. He'd decide what to do in the morning, he said, when he saw what the weather was like.

Although a cloudy dawn didn't seem too promising he announced he was heading for Cataract Pass the next morning. Packing an un-comfortable-looking framed rucksack, which appeared to be held together with string with most of his belongings tied to the outside, he announced that he was an experienced walker but that he usually only undertook day trips. He hated backpacking because the pack was so awkward to carry. With the badly-packed, badly-designed pack he had I could well believe it and the thought of him trying to carry that unstable load whilst wearing smooth-soled shoes over the route I'd walked the day before made me shudder. But he was determined to go on and set off up the trail with the pack swaying on his back watched with concern by me and one of the other campers, Al from Ontario. We discussed his chances of making it and decided they were slim. I never heard of any accidents in the area, though, and I did check when I reached Jasper so I presume he made it out to the road somehow. Meeting him did make me aware that there are skills involved in backpacking that have to be learned and that it's easy to be uncomfortable.

For the next 45 miles I was on The Glacier Trail which runs from the Nigel Pass trailhead on the Icefields Parkway, where the man with no boots had begun, to Maligne Lake via a series of valleys linked by high passes. This is part of a route first undertaken by outfitter Jack Brewster in 1924 that went from Jasper to Lake Louise. Paved roads occupy most of the route today but the central high level section still remains for the walker to enjoy. I began this spectacular trail by dropping down through the forest for a few miles to the Four Point Campground where there were several tents. Here I turned up the Four Point Valley on a climb the *Trail Guide* described as 'vigorous' (650 feet in just over a mile) and which soon brought me above timberline. A cold wind with a hint of rain was sweeping down the valley and the sheet-grey of the sky cast a dull light over the scenery so I was hurrying along not noticing much when I glimpsed something moving away to my right.

I turned and there, a few hundred feet away, was a large pale-coloured grizzly bear heading towards me. I felt stunned, scared and elated in quick succession. Fear was my dominant emotion though for the bear was huge and getting closer by the second. I'd stopped on seeing it and quickly realised it was unaware of my presence. The wind was whipping my scent away down the valley and the noise of the creek that lay between me and the bear meant it hadn't heard me. I soon remedied the latter by putting on a quite ridiculous performance that I hoped no distant hiker was watching. I jumped up and down, clapping my hands, shouting and blowing on my safety whistle. The bear stopped momentarily, raised its muzzle and moved its head slowly from side to side sniffing the air before changing its direction slightly and moving off down the creek. Feeling greatly relieved I moved up the hillside above the trail a short distance then took off my pack and set up my tripod and camera, determined to take a few photographs of the bear, however bad they might be. I was glad now I'd brought a 70-210 telephoto zoom lens and a 2x converter as I didn't want to get very close. I was uncomfortably aware that the only two deaths from grizzly attacks the previous year that I knew of had been of photographers approaching too close to the bears. For half an hour I watched as the grizzly rippled effortlessly along beside the creek, turning over rocks and rooting in corners. I felt very privileged to see this magnificent beast at home in the mountains, the very epitome of wilderness. I also felt alarmed at seeing the bear vanish into the willow thickets that lined the creek and trail in places. How often had I been close to a bear without realising it?

Feeling inspired by my encounter with the grizzly I strode on over Jonas Pass and then up steeply to 8100-foot Jonas Shoulder Summit where the trail crosses the narrow rocky ridge between the Jonas and Poboktan Creek valleys. Here I caught up with another hiker whom I'd seen ahead of me heading upwards. He hadn't seen the bear. After he'd gone on I climbed up above the narrow notch where the trail ran to gaze out over the peaks of the Front Ranges. Returning to my pack I found a small ground squirrel sitting on it gnawing a hole through the side pocket containing my trail mix. Approaching slowly and quietly I managed to get near enough to take a photograph before the squirrel sensed my presence and scurried off.

From the ridge I dropped back down to timberline and the Jonas Cutoff Campground where I found two tents already pitched. One belonged to an American couple who were heading over Jonas Shoulder the next day. On hearing about the bear they said I should talk to the other hiker as he'd met it too. I wandered over to his tent and mentioned the grizzly. 'Oh yes, the bear,' he said, looking rather wild. 'Well, I met four of them!' He'd been at Four Point Campground the previous evening and on leaving had seen a female grizzly with two cubs in the forest not far from the site. They'd run off as soon as they saw him. Then near where I'd met the bear he'd seen what he thought was a marmot on the trail ahead. But when he'd come over a short rise he'd found a grizzly coming towards him just fifty feet away. The 'marmot' had been the bear's hump! As the bear kept walking towards him he'd left the trail and descended to the creek and begun to walk up alongside it only for the bear also to drop down to the creek and again walk towards him. So he'd returned to the trail. Luckily this time the bear didn't follow him but stayed by the creek. It must have been the same bear I met just an hour or so later. In seven years of walking in the Rockies my fellow camper had only seen four bears and now he'd doubled that total in a few hours. I could see the effect the encounters had had on him as he looked quite shocked and kept muttering 'four bears, four bears', as if he didn't quite believe what had happened. It certainly put my bear encounter into perspective.

The rain which had been threatening all day began at 11pm. It was still falling steadily at dawn and continued all the next day, the wettest day for three weeks and the start of an unsettled period of weather that was to last for the same period of time. The date was August 1st. 'You take your chance coming to the Rockies in August,' read *The Handbook,* 'In some years . . . a succession of Pacific low-pressure systems has kept the Rockies soggy and cool.' This was to be one of those years. The Americans Bill and Sue decided to head out via Poboktan Creek rather than tackle the high passes as did two women hikers who'd arrived late the previous evening. This was my route anyway. The trail was very muddy and slippery, quite the worst I'd come across. I met a trail crew at work who told me the reason was the trail's popularity with horse parties. The trail leader, Rick, was a friend of Ben Gadd. 'Bet you'd like some fresh food,' he said when I told him about my walk. He was right. We wandered down to the warden cabin where he loaded me up with carrots, plums, apples and a carton of apricot yoghurt. 'We live in luxury here,' he said, 'all the supplies come in by helicopter.' He also told me that there was a restaurant at Maligne Lake which was something to look forward to as I plugged on through the mud past several roaring waterfalls. As I continued the descent I heard ahead what sounded like a motor vehicle then rounded a corner in the trail to see a mini-bulldozer blocking the way. At this point the trail was only a foot wide and cut into a steep bank, on the far side of which the bulldozer was digging a path wide enough for its tracks. The driver was another part of the trail crew. 'What we're actually doing is building a small road, though officially it's a trail,' he said, 'with a hardened surface and drainage channels. It's for all the horses.' He was supposed to drive the vehicle right up the valley but as he had to make a track for it as he went along, progress was slow and he doubted he'd get there before the summer was over. Soon afterwards I came to a trail junction and I left the Poboktan Creek Trail to follow Poligne Creek, the crossings of which I was glad to find bridged (despite what the *Trail Guide* said), up to the flower meadows of 7340-foot Maligne Pass where fresh wet snow lay on the ground, the first I'd seen for nearly two months. A cold wind swept the open pass and I didn't linger. A wide muddy swathe slashed across the meadows looked as if someone had been practising cavalry charges across it. The whole area was cut up badly by horses' hooves.

Down in the upper Maligne Valley, Mary Vaux Campground sported a couple of wet tents and some wet people cooking food under the trees. I talked to two women who listened to my plans in disbelief. You won't make it, they said, summer's nearly over, the winter snows will start soon. Once it's August I start thinking of skiing, said one. I could only hope they were wrong.

Clearing skies came with the dawn and by noon it was sunny. The trail was less muddy and all in all I had a much more enjoyable day as I walked the nineteen miles down to Maligne Lake. Where the forest opened out into meadows I could see fresh snow plastering the peaks above. Maligne Lake, the longest in the Canadian Rockies at 14 miles, is one of the classic beauty spots, the view down the lake featuring in calendars, postcards and posters of the region. It's also a popular tourist destination as a road runs up to the north shore where there are cabins, a lodge, a restaurant and boat hiring facilities. The first European to visit the lake was Mary Schaffer in 1908 who on the same trip crossed Maligne Pass. She then spent several more summers exploring the Rockies with her friends Mollie Adams and Mary Vaux. Her entertaining stories of these trips, first published in 1911, have been reprinted in a book entitled *A Hunter of Peace*. I bought another book about the early exploration of the Rockies in the Maligne Lake gift shop, William Taylor's *Tracks Across My Trail*, which tells the story of Donald 'Curly' Phillips who built the still-standing boathouse on the lake and became the leading outfitter in Jasper National Park before being killed in an avalanche in 1938. As well as reading matter I bought some rolls, slices of cake and little cartons of butter and cheese from the café for the next few days' breakfasts as I was out of cereal. After 40 days and 480 miles my appetite was growing rapidly and I knew I would have to boost my supplies if I was not to go hungry.

From Maligne Lake the Skyline Trail runs for 27 miles almost to Jasper townsite. As 25 of those miles are either on or above timberline, more than on any other trail, it is a popular and highly rated route. Indeed in *The Handbook* Ben Gadd describes it as 'the best hike in the Rockies'. Leaving the lake I ambled up the first three miles of the trail to the Evelyn Creek Campground where I found two Dutch backpackers camped. They were the only people I met who weren't impressed by the Rockies. 'Too much walking in woods,' said one. They'd spent the previous two summers in the open expanses of Iceland which they said they much preferred. Unfortunately just as they were starting on the Skyline Trail where they would have been out of the trees, one of them had twisted her knee so they were going back down the next day. They weren't bothering hanging their food as there was no pole, their logic being that no pole meant no bears. I camped away from them and hung my food anyway. After my bear encounter I was taking no risks.

High cirrus late in the evening suggested the start of another front and sure enough I was woken at 5am by rain. By 9am this had dwindled to intermittent drizzle but the cloud was still thick and low. I noted *The Handbook's* other comment on the Skyline Trail: 'in bad weather it is the worst hike in the Rockies' but went, as I had to, anyway, though I held off my departure until 11.30 by which time a few patches of blue sky had appeared. The delay was worthwhile as by the time I reached 7350-foot Little Shovel Pass the clouds were lifting. En route to the pass I'd met a couple from Ontario packing up at the Little Shovel campsite and they caught me up as I rested at the top before descending into a vast alpine amphitheatre called the Snowbowl where beautiful flower meadows spread as far as the eye could see. On a bank on the edge of the meadows we found a ptarmigan with two young which were very tame, enabling us to take photographs from close quarters.

Across the Snowbowl the trail climbed to Shovel Pass itself at 7610 feet. Just before I reached the pass I saw a herd of animals far away on the open mountainside. Through the binoculars I identified them as caribou, an animal I was to become very familiar with towards the end of the walk, though this first sighting left me feeling very pleased as I knew there weren't many of these arctic tundra animals (the North American equivalent of the reindeer) this far south. Shovel Pass' unusual name relates to an actual incident which occurred in 1911 when two pioneer outfitters from Jasper, the Otto brothers, attempted to drag a boat to Maligne Lake via this route. Deep snow meant their horses couldn't cross the pass so they'd made shovels out of the stunted trees growing here and dug a trail through the snow.

A long, climbing traverse across barren slopes led above the blue waters of Curator Lake to the start of the steep, rocky ascent to The Notch, a narrow gap leading onto the summit ridge of Amber Mountain. Ahead two tiny dots marked a pair of hikers near the top of the climb. At 8235 feet The Notch is the high point of the Skyline Trail and a superb viewpoint for the Main Ranges to the west across the Athabasca River valley. A profusion of spires, domes, towers, glaciers and icefields stretched north and south, the heartland of the Canadian Rockies containing the highest peaks and the biggest snowfields. Far below I could see the thin silver thread of the river winding through the dark blanket of the forest. For three miles the trail stays at around 8200 feet giving superlative views all around. A strong wind hampered my attempts at capturing the scene on film but by bracing myself against boulders I managed to take a couple of shots.

Ahead lay the great cliffs of Mount Tekarra below which I began the descent on a snaking, switchbacking trail to Centre and Tekarra Lakes and another timberline camp at Tekarra Campground. On the way down I caught up with the two walkers I'd seen ahead of me, one of whom turned out to be from England. They were going on to the next site having started at the one below Curator Lake. I stopped at Tekarra. I could have gone further but the next site was deep in the forest whilst this one gave good views. From here I knew I could reach Jasper townsite in half a day anyway. A gusty breeze kept the mosquitos away, which was another reason for staying at Tekarra. Again I had company. Three walkers from Switzerland were camped nearby and there was another tent further away whose occupants I didn't see. There was no bear pole and again I was the only person to hang his food, little though I had.

Another front blew in overnight, waking me at half past midnight with a blast of rain and wind. I hadn't set the storm guys but the tent held up well and I felt quite secure. The dawn clouds were pink-tinged and the rain had ceased by 6am though the wind blew on. I didn't mind. I was heading down. Four hours after I set off on the long, wooded, sweaty, humid descent I was in Jasper. I collected my mail, which included a new rain jacket as well as my supply box and a bundle of letters, and did a bit of shopping before heading for Ben and Cia Gadd's. In the town I met the couple from the day before. They'd finished their walk and were heading back to Vancouver where one of them, Bruce, lived. Early in 1989 I received a letter from Rachel Kilbey, the English half of the couple who lived in Chorley, saying that they wanted to do a section of the Great Divide Trail in the summer and could I give them any advice. 'I suppose you could say you inspired us!' she wrote. They'd traced me though Ben Gadd, with whom I'd told them I was going to stay.

I very much wanted to meet Ben having corresponded with him and lived with his book for so long. Also he was the main inspiration for this walk. When I found his house I was welcomed in and made to feel very much at home and we found we had much in common and much to talk about. Soon after my arrival Ben and Cia very politely suggested I had a bath and then washed my clothes. It was only after the bath and in a set of fresh, loaned clothes that I realised just how much my own clothes stank. These were clearly tolerant people!

Ben, a geologist by training, currently works as an independent licensed interpretative naturalist in Jasper National Park, taking people out into the mountains. He has lived in or near the Rockies all his life and his deep love for the region came over strongly whilst talking to him, as it does in his book. *The Handbook,* I was pleased to hear, had been a great success, already going into its third edition. In order to bring it out in the form he wanted, Ben had ended up publishing and distributing the book himself.

I discussed my proposed route with Ben who suggested I modify the next section to see more of the Front Ranges. He and Cia also put me in touch with a local outfitter, Rocky Notnes, who worked in the Willmore Wilderness Park, north of Jasper, and who gave me some up-to-date information on the state of the trails there and recommended a route through the area which I took, and which made the next fortnight's travel much easier than it otherwise would have been. Ben also phoned the

Mount Robson Provincial Park who confirmed that they'd taken my supply box up to their Berg Lake warden cabin for me. They also said that a route into the park I'd been unable to find any information on was an 'easy bushwhack'. I now had a new route that would keep me on trails for longer than my original one would have done.

The day after I arrived in Jasper was one of torrential rain and I spent it shopping and talking to Ben and Cia and Cia's mother. My revised route meant I would be going to the town of Grande Cache rather than Prince George where my supplies were, but I couldn't do anything about this as it was a weekend and the post offices were closed. Cia offered to try and arrange for my mail to be forwarded on the Monday by which time I would be well on my way.

The rain continued but I had to go, so the next day I set off, making it just 4 miles to the large roadside Wapiti Campground. I was well-placed for an early start the next morning though. My pack was very heavy. I probably had too much food for my revised route but was loath to leave any behind in case it turned out to take longer than I thought.

The Highest Mountain and The Longest Trail

Jasper to Grande Cache
8th to 23rd August 236 miles

I was very conscious as I ate a large and excellent breakfast in the Jasper House restaurant down the road from the campground, that this was the last meal I wouldn't make myself for at least two weeks (seventeen days as it turned out), as I had before me a section where my only resupply point was the Mount Robson Provincial Park backcountry warden station at Berg Lake to which one of my supply boxes had been transported. Yet my northward progress would be very little during this period as I would be making a large loop out west and back again, crossing the Great Divide three times. In fact I started by heading south-west! There were various reasons for this convoluted route. If a direct line had been my main aim I'd simply have headed north from Jasper to Grande Cache and been there in less than a week. Straight lines were not important though; experiencing the best the Rockies had to offer was; and west of Jasper lay The Ramparts, rated in *The Handbook* as 'the grandest place in the park and perhaps in the entire Canadian Rockies' (though the *Trail Guide* says that when the rain is pelting down in mid-summer 'this lovely area comes very close to a backpacker's definition of hell'). Moreover north of them was Mount Robson, the highest peak in the range. I very much wanted to visit both these places and had planned my route to include them. Because my new supply point of Grande Cache lay on the eastern edge of the mountains I now had to head back in that direction from the Robson area.

My westward trek began up the Marmot Basin Ski Area road under clearing skies. I stopped for a snack at the Portal Creek campground and watched fascinated whilst the only other person there, a check-shirted man with a campavan, forced long, freshly cut green branches into an already packed firepit to produce clouds of smoke but not much else. He seemed quite happy in this occupation and ignored me completely. As I continued the climb I could see across the Athabasca River valley, Mount Tekarra

70

plastered with fresh snow and the mountain crest along which the Skyline Trail ran. As the day warmed up and the sun came out the snow almost visibly melted. It was the nicest day for a week. Leaving the tarmac for the Tonquin Valley Trail I climbed up the narrow valley, known appropriately as The Portal, and crossed some large rockslides before reaching the Portal Creek campsite. Here I had problems finding anywhere to pitch the tent for the site was waterlogged with large puddles remaining surrounded by the deep scars of hastily-made drainage ditches. Much litter including food scraps and a whole sodden toilet roll suggested that the last campers had made a rapid retreat. As was becoming the norm, I lit a fire and burnt the rubbish, cutting up the provided logs with a bow saw chained to a tree, a feature I hadn't encountered at any other site. For supper I ate a 'Retort' meal of cabbage rolls, one of two Ben had given me to try. This fresh food in a sealed pack was much tastier than my dried meals but quite heavy for the amount of food provided. I wouldn't have been prepared to carry two weeks' worth of it but an occasional Retort meal was nice.

The good weather didn't last and I woke to clouds and a strong wind blowing down from Maccarib Pass where I was heading. Flurries of drizzle accompanied the wind and I set up the tarp before having breakfast. A pika watched me eating from a nearby rockpile. Pikas are little grey furry animals related to rabbits, though they look more like hamsters, that live in boulder fields above timberline.

A party of four climbers who'd been staying in the Alpine Club of Canada hut at Amethyst Lakes stopped to chat as I neared Maccarib Pass and turned out to be Yoho National Park staff. It was only after they'd gone that I realised I should have given them a message for Shirley Green. On a high shoulder beyond the grey windswept pass I saw a herd of animals moving slowly uphill. Through the binoculars I could see they were caribou, nineteen in all. I watched them for some time, delighted to have seen a second herd of these creatures. The wildlife was making up for the weather.

Near Amethyst Lakes I met a warden riding out, huddled under his cape against the increasingly cold blasts of storm. Further on a long string of horse riders passed me, a party from the outfitters' cabins that lie along the lakeshore. The appalling state of the trail where unsightly wooden duckboards were mixed with stretches of deep, churned-up clinging mud had already shown me that heavy horse traffic was common here. Although I'd only walked ten miles I decided to stop at the Amethyst Lakes campsite in the hope that the weather would clear and I would have a view of The Ramparts, the great rock wall that lay on the far side of the lakes. After adding several days of walking to my journey in order to visit this area it seemed worthwhile staying here a short time. Even in the cloud the cliffs rising out of the dark, wind-ruffled waters of the lakes were impressive.

Again there was much litter and food waste at the site, though no other campers, and I spent some time cleaning it up. I pitched the tent in the partial shelter of a large boulder and some scrubby trees but with a good view across the lake to the cliffs. Two German walkers passed by heading for Maccarib Pass as I wandered down to the lake where I watched a magnificent common loon (British great northern diver) swimming and diving near the shore. These dark birds with their distinctive white throat necklaces swim tens of metres underwater after they dive and I spent some time trying to guess where it would surface each time it dived. I was never right. Then I was distracted as farther down the lake a bald eagle soared low over the water.

I returned to the site to find four fishermen from Chicago setting up camp and trying to light a fire, an endeavour in which they had little success as it began to rain heavily, though I could hear the clunk of their axe all evening. Two Japanese walkers turned up as I cowered under the tarp cooking supper and asked if this was the site. On learning it was, they retreated into the woods to pitch their tent. A wise move as the wind rose and I began to wonder if I'd made a mistake in going for a scenic rather than a well-sheltered pitch. Bells in the meadow turned out to belong to the outfitters' horses, turned loose to graze. All afternoon and evening the sound of stonefall echoed across the lake from The Ramparts. Yet despite the weather and the noise and people, the place had a tranquil air about it.

The storm raged throughout the night, waking me several times, but the tent held firm. I woke in the morning to an unusual sensation of insecurity. The ground under the tent moved when I did and I felt as though I was lying on a waterbed. In a sense I was, for when I lifted the edge of the groundsheet and peered under it, a large pool of water slopped lazily about. Kneeling in the entrance I drained it away via a trench dug with my plastic toilet trowel. Amazingly the groundsheet hadn't leaked. Squalls of hail and rain were blasting through the campsite every few minutes but in between them shafts of sunshine would split the clouds and rainbows would curve over the turbulent sparkling waters of the lake. I set the camera up on the tripod under the tarp and dashed out to take pictures between each burst of rain. In this weather I was in no hurry to leave and read my way through the morning. Two Swiss walkers passed by trying to hold down their flapping ponchos. They considered the site but decided to head for a lower, more sheltered one. The range of nationalities I was meeting here was a sign of just how famous The Ramparts are.

After lunch I finally conceded that the weather was not going to improve so I packed up and left in the now continuous pouring rain. The trail had become a sticky, slippery quagmire. I was heading for Moat Pass and entry into British Columbia for the first time since Howse Pass which I'd crossed in similar conditions a fortnight earlier. At the pass I also entered Mount Robson Provincial Park and began the descent of the Tonquin Creek valley which the park staff had told Ben Gadd in Jasper was an 'easy bushwhack'. Moat Lake, just before the pass, was a wild and beautiful place with The Ramparts rising into the mist above the far shore. The going, down the wide and marshy upper valley, was easy though the ground soon started to steepen. I stopped when I found a place that was flat and dry enough for a camp. Now I was no longer in a national park I could camp where I liked. Hanging my food sacks was difficult though and I missed the bear poles. It took an hour before I had the line over a branch that didn't break. Then I discovered that I'd lost my bob hat. I'd tucked it into my belt when I'd dropped out of the cold winds on the pass as I was too lazy to remove my pack and put it safely away. As it was red in colour I thought I might spot it if I looked for it so I spent an hour or so searching for it. However as I wasn't on a trail I couldn't retrace my route exactly and eventually gave up without finding it. Luckily I had a headover, a tube of material designed to be worn round the neck, that could be used as a hat, but I still made a note to buy another hat when I could. The evenings were cool enough now to need one.

The dawn temperature of 4°C was not low enough to keep away the hordes of mosquitos that were massed for attack outside the condensation-sodden tent. The bugs plagued me throughout the four-hour-long desperate descent to the Fraser River. I stumbled, fell and fought through dense vegetation, over tangled networks of fallen trees and down steep, loose earth and rock slopes. The air was hot and humid, I was soaked in sweat and insect repellent, bloody with scratches, sore from bruises and filthy with mud and dirt. I was kept going by the hatred I felt welling up for the park staff and their 'easy bushwhack'. Finally the hillside began to level out and a thrash through some tightly packed trees brought me to the side of the river and the remains of a trail. I was so exhausted that I rested for an hour and a half and for the first time on the walk lit the stove during the day and made and drank three pint-mugfuls of coffee in quick succession.

The park staff were spared further maledictions, as the old trapper's trail they'd said led down the river valley and out to the Yellowhead Highway was actually there and, although unmaintained, still in reasonable condition. As this trail stayed in the forest and away from the river there were no views, so I pushed on at a fast pace, making a fair amount of noise as fresh bear dung littered the trail. In a few places old rusted traps hung from trees and I passed an abandoned cabin. Peering in through a broken window I could see torn mattresses and sleeping bags, old clothes, unopened tin cans, a paraffin lamp, some paperback books and various tools and other items. Animal and bird droppings were everywhere. It looked as though someone had left one day intending to return but for some reason had never come back, leaving the cabin to the animals.

There were many animal signs, both tracks and droppings, on the path too. I liked the fact that this trail, built in order to kill wildlife, had now been taken over by them as a route. If they hadn't done so, the trail would have been heavily overgrown and much tougher to walk. As I neared the road, signs that people had been along it recently appeared with fresh blazes on trees. Curving away from the river and over the shoulder of a hill the trail ended with a steep climb which I did in growing darkness, the red ball of the setting sun visible through the black branches of the closely-packed trees, before dropping down abruptly to the highway and the Lucerne Campground where I was lucky in grabbing the one empty site at a cost of $7. I didn't feel sorry for those I saw being turned away; they had vehicles and would soon be at the next site. I'd walked 22 miles despite the awful start and just wanted to sleep. Even the inevitable mad axeman chopping away in the darkness couldn't keep me awake.

The campground warden told me that the forecast was for a few days of good weather and the chilly dawn and clear sky told of a hot day to come. To reach the next trailhead I had a 12-mile westward road walk which I wasn't looking forward to, the Yellowhead Highway being a major east-west crossing. My plan to do it as fast as possible fell apart however as I encountered a series of work crews laying telephone cables beside the highway. As I passed each one, someone would come over and ask me what I was doing and where I was going. By the fourth or fifth one I felt like a tape recorder. Press the button and out came the story. The only point of interest was what park wardens call an 'animal jam'. I first saw a number of vehicles parked on the hard shoulders either side of the highway, which isn't allowed, and thought there'd been an accident. Then I saw that people were hurrying back and forth quite recklessly across the tarmac and that most of them were carrying cameras, everything from giant video monsters to pocket-size compacts. The reason became apparent as I drew near and saw two magnificent elk stags grazing in the grass by the road totally oblivious of the chaos they were causing. I soon had my camera out too—this was the closest I'd been to an elk stag.

Finally I reached the roadhead for the Moose River Trail which I wanted to follow to Mount Robson. The *Trail Guide* warned of major stream crossings and a poorly marked and in places overgrown trail but said it was 'a highly scenic option for experienced backpackers'. If I didn't merit the latter description by now I never would, so along the trail I went, heartened by a map in a glass case at the start on which were marked a number of 'hiker/horse' camps. I was encouraged even more by the discovery of very recent trail maintenance and blazing. A few sections had even been completely recut and people on foot and on horseback had been along it recently. After $10^{1}/2$ miles I reached the first major ford, that of Resplendent Creek. As I approached the river's edge a flash of brown had me staring up into a tree. A sharp-eyed pine marten stared back before vanishing upwards. By the side of the wide, multi-channelled and glacier-melt grey creek was a good, if well-used and garbage-strewn, site on which I camped. The ford was described in the *Trail Guide* as 'difficult', the creek often deep, with the run-off from the glaciers on Mount Robson's southern slopes, so I decided to cross it early in the morning when it would be at its lowest.

The night was frosty, as I found when I woke in the blackness to find my self-inflating mattress had deflated itself, lowering me gently to the hard, cold ground. I found the leak, which, unfortunately, was along a seam near the valve, an awkward place for a repair, but I patched it as best I could. I'd barely returned to sleep when I was woken by an eerie, odd up-and-down-the-scale repetitive cry. With no idea what was making the noise I peered cautiously out of the tent. A porcupine looked at me from a few feet away and uttered the strange call again. As it wouldn't go away when I made a noise and threw things at it but just stared at me I had to throw on some clothes, leave the tent and pursue it across the site until it retreated into the depths of some dense bushes. By dawn it had recovered sufficiently from this ordeal to be back by my tent happily devouring a bandana. I was beginning to dislike porcupines.

The morning was clear and still. I could hear the sound of traffic and trains in the Yellowhead valley six or so miles away. Resplendent Creek turned out to be no more than ankle deep but I couldn't find the trail on the far side. The forest was dense and there was a steep ridge to climb so I really wanted to find the trail which I knew was there somewhere. I left the pack and prospected up and down the bank with no success, just a scare when I couldn't locate the pack where I thought I'd left it. Once I did find it I shouldered it immediately. I'd rather have had no trail than no pack. Two hours of frustrating bushwhacking passed before I realised on consulting the map that the trail lay nearly a mile upstream, farther than I'd searched. I headed up the bank to the spot marked on the map and there was the trail, marked by a white metal triangle nailed to a tree so that people crossing the creek could find it. It hadn't occurred to me to consult the map at first. So much for being an experienced backpacker! At least the sun was shining.

I crossed the intervening wooded ridge and descended back down to the Moose River itself and a trail that dodged in and out of the trees giving many excellent views to the Mount Mackray group across the river. The *Trail Guide* said there were four fords of the river to do in the space of three miles. The water, although sluggish, looked deep so when I came to the first ford I decided I'd simply bushwhack along the bank until the trail crossed back. It wasn't a day for being independent though. A short distance further and I found out why there was a ford as I sank knee deep into a particularly glutinous, reeking swamp. Now both my boots and my running shoes, which I'd used for the Resplendent Creek crossing, were soaked. From now on I would stick to the trail.

I arrived feeling very fed up and cold at a campsite on a spit of land between Steppe Creek and the Moose River at 9.15pm after a long, tiring day during which I'd only progressed 12 miles. In the last hour of the walk I'd had six fords to cross, three of the river and three of Steppe Creek, and I'd felt the evening cold closing in especially as I was walking in the shadow of the high peaks to the west. For the first time on the walk I lit a fire for warmth before I set up camp.

Two white-tailed deer were staring at me when I stuck my head out of the tent into the sharp, dawn air. They soon retreated, unlike the mosquitos. Any skill I possessed in trail finding continued to elude me again as I searched for the path beyond the final ford of Steppe Creek for one and a half hours. This time a false horse trail led me far upstream before fading away. Inevitably it seemed, the true trail lay in the other direction. Once I'd located it I followed it to Moose Pass and a return across the Divide into Alberta and Jasper National Park. There were beautiful purple and blue lupin meadows all around the pass but there was also a cold wind whipping spots of rain into my face and dark clouds rolling in from the west, so I didn't linger but hurried down by Calumet Creek. The final obstacle on the Moose River Trail then faced me, the Coleman Glacier outflow creek. 'This wide silty torrent is best forded downstream where it is braided,' said the *Trail Guide,* going on to describe the crossing as hazardous. I looked at the grey, roaring waters swirling down in front of me and took the book's advice. Even then it took some time to find safe ways across the different channels, making this a difficult ford requiring much care. I was very relieved when I climbed out onto the far bank and bushwhacked up to a trail. I headed off down this trail looking for the junction with the North Boundary Trail which I would follow a short distance to a campground, but I couldn't find it. I roamed up and down the trail for an hour as the light faded, before sitting down with the map to work it out. For the third time in two days I'd made a mistake. I was already on the North Boundary Trail and had misread the

Trail Guide. I'd not only forded the outflow creek but also the Smoky River though I hadn't realised it and had been looking for the bridge over the Smoky that would lead to the North Boundary Trail. Now going in the right direction I rounded a bend in the trail to be greeted by the majestic sight of Mount Robson, highest in the Canadian Rockies, rising into pink clouds above the flat meadows of Adolphus Pass. It was 9pm and nearly dark and I was very tired, but I still had to stop and take a photograph.

Adolphus Campground where I stopped for the night was deserted. Indeed I'd seen no-one since leaving the highway. As I sat by my fire I relished the silence and solitude for I knew that little more than a mile away lay Berg Lake, the most popular backcountry destination in the Canadian Rockies, where I would be the next day, along, no doubt, with many others.

Mount Robson was shrouded in cloud the next morning as I crossed the broad, flat expanse of 5420-foot Robson Pass to be greeted by a swathe of Black's Good Companions tents, a model familiar to anyone who started camping in the sixties, lying across the flats at the end of Berg Lake. This, as I found out later, was the summer camp of the Alpine Club of Canada. I wandered past the rows of canvas to Rearguard Campground, one of three that lie along Berg Lake, where I stopped and set up camp. Amazingly no-one else was there.

Even though the summit was hidden behind a solid grey blanket of cloud, the view of Mount Robson across the lake was impressive. From out of the tattered lower edge of the cloud appeared the two tumbling icefalls of Mist Glacier and Berg Glacier slipping ever so slowly into the lake waters. During my stay here I was to grow used to the constant grinding and grumbling of the moving ice and the occasional crash of an iceberg calving off into the lake. The scale is immense with the 12,972-foot summit of Robson being more than a mile and a quarter above the lake.

Mount Robson was first climbed by an ACC party led by guide Conrad Kain in 1913 after several earlier attempts. The most interesting of these was that of the Rev. Kinney and outfitter Curly Philips, whom we've already met as the builder of the Maligne Lake boathouse. The latter had only just arrived in the Rockies from Ontario and had never climbed a mountain when he was hired by Kinney to guide him on Robson. Despite this the two very nearly reached the top with Kinney saying that they did so, though this claim was later discounted. Curly Philips went on to become a successful outfitter and in 1913 he built the first trail from the Robson River up to Berg Lake in preparation for that year's ACC summer camp. 1988's camp was supplied by helicopter but Philips' 11-mile trail from the highway at the Robson River is still the most popular way to Berg Lake and the most used trail in the Rockies.

Even with today's equipment, climbing Robson is difficult. Ben Gadd, who has made two ascents by different routes, describes the climb in *The Handbook* as 'a mini-expedition for experienced climbers. Plan to spend a week on the mountain'. I had no dreams of climbing the peak, at least not on this trip, but I did think that a walk along the Canadian Rockies should include a visit to the highest peak.

The park wardens having kindly brought in a food parcel for me, this was the only supply point on the route actually in the backcountry. Once I'd set up camp and hung my food I set off to the warden's cabin to collect my supplies. Due to the attentions of the local rodents they had been repacked for me by the warden into some metal containers. For my original off-trail route I'd packed sixteen days' worth of food. However now I was going to Grande Cache I only needed half that amount so I left some with the warden and some more at the ACC camp.

In the hope that Mount Robson would appear out of the clouds I decided to stay an extra day even though I'd only walked a couple of miles the day I'd arrived. At least seeing Robson was my excuse. Once I'd made the decision, though, I felt very relieved and realised that the eight days' walk from Jasper with all the bushwhacking, river fords and stormy weather had left me feeling quite tired. I needed a rest.

Down at the main Berg Lake Campground where there was a day cabin for cooking and drying out wet gear, I found all the people. Tents were everywhere with those of a sixteen-strong German party occupying much of the site. With steady rain falling and no views I spent most of my rest day in the warmth of the shelter talking to the steady stream of walkers and climbers who came in. The visitors varied from fast walkers, who were doing the round trip from the roadhead in a day, to alpine mountaineers waiting for the weather to clear. Few were intending to go much further than a day-walk or climb. A mother and son team arrived, the son being keen on 'survival' which meant cutting boughs for a bed and erecting a tarp for shelter. I wasn't sure how well he'd survive the wrath of the wardens if they found out what he was doing. So heavy is the use here that even camp fires are banned, the idea being that the wood stove in the shelter can be used for warmth and cooking, fuel being brought in by helicopter, so that the local trees can remain uncut. There are no bear poles either, food being stored in chests in the cabin. Yet just a third of a mile away I had Rearguard Campground with firepits and bear pole to myself.

Although most people walk in, some don't, and those of us in the cabin were surprised to hear a helicopter arrive just outside during the afternoon. Rushing to the door we saw a large party of Japanese hikers with vast amounts of gear alighting from the large and noisy machine. They were watched with envy that night as they cooked up delicious smelling fresh meals in large woks that seemed in danger of overbalancing on the tiny backpacking stoves they were using. Luxury in the wilderness indeed! Personally I'd rather walk in and eat dried food and do without the intrusion of the helicopters.

The second surprise of the day came in the evening when two of the ACC guides brought over a generator and a projector and screen and gave a slide show on Mount Robson! The pictures were interesting, showing what we couldn't see outside, but it was bizarre to sit and look at slides of Robson with the mountain itself only a short distance away. When slides of the Berg Glacier came up I could look out of the window at the real thing! The show over I walked back in the dark to my tent and nearly fell over a porcupine which I think was even more startled than I was. A wrestle with the still deflating sleeping mat in the middle of the night resulted in my changing the valve and spreading liberal quantities of glue over the interior of the tent. It still went down again.

Further rain and low clouds the morning after the slide show didn't prevent me leaving. I'd had enough of the Berg Lake circus. I was now heading east back into Jasper National Park and Alberta along the North Boundary Trail. Because it leads to Mount Robson this trail is usually walked in the other direction so I was to meet many backpackers along it. The NBT is a popular trail not because it's particularly scenic, which it isn't ('much . . . is in boring valley bottoms' *(The Handbook)*, 'many travellers find the trail quite tedious' *(Trail Guide)*), but because it's a 108-mile through route. The distance makes it one of the longest single trails in the Canadian Rockies and therefore a goal for many walkers who spend from a week to a fortnight on it. Ben Gadd had told me that he'd done it once on a mountain bike, and that runners had traversed it in just a few days. Most folk walk however. Only on the NBT did I meet other people who regarded themselves as long-distance backpackers. People like long footpaths. It's easier to say one has done The North Boundary Trail or The Pennine Way or The Tour of Mont Blanc than to say you've walked between two places no-one has ever heard of (such as Waterton Lakes and Liard River!). The name and distance tells other walkers what you have achieved. After two days at Berg Lake explaining exactly where I'd come from (I was surprised at how few people, even Canadians, had heard of Waterton Lakes National Park) and where I was going I'd have appreciated a simple name for my walk like The Canadian Rockies Trail. Berg Lake is 'a fitting terminus to the Great Divide Trail' according to the *Trail Guide* so I suppose I'd walked a version of this. The name hasn't caught the imagination of many backpackers however and when I tried it out on a few along the NBT they were very unsure as to what it was, even though they were nearly all carrying the guide.

Within hours of recrossing Robson Pass I met three NBT parties slogging through the mud. First came four rather grim Germans, then three similarly dour Canadians followed by a cheerful solo Scot who told me he now lived in Canada. When I asked why, he just waved his hand at the mountains. No further explanation was needed. He was aiming at finishing the trail in a week—unlike the other parties who were taking twice as long. Perhaps that's why he wasn't miserable. The tired, bedraggled, depressed walkers were typical of those I've met on every well-known long distance path I've ever walked. You can meet hundreds like them every day on the Pennine Way in summer. The cachet of walking a famous route seems to attract many who don't really possess the experience to enjoy the walk, but who complete the challenge on willpower alone, with only the satisfaction of success as a reward.

A thunderstorm brought heavy rain which passed in twenty minutes though the sky remained dark. The Wolverine Campground loomed up and I decided to stop. Ann and John, a sister and brother who lived locally, were lighting a fire in the only firepit as I arrived, and I joined them round the warm blaze as soon as I'd set up camp. This was Ann's first backpacking trip and the first for many years for John, who was the older of the two. They'd already learnt a lot about technique and talked about what they'd do differently next year when they planned walking the South Boundary Trail, a walk of similar length but a more difficult route, at the other end of the park. They had some unusual gear including bulky, heavy metallic-lined synthetic-filled sleeping bags. 'Like sleeping in baco foil; you need long underwear or else it sticks to you,' said John. The items they said were most inadequate, though, were their packs. Neither of their pack frames had padded hip belts and John's was twenty years old. They'd have new ones for their next trip, they said. Like me, they did, though, have a tarp to use as a cooking shelter, the only people I met on the whole walk who had one.

They had blisters too, as I discovered the next morning when I watched them bandage up their feet before heading off. They were wearing heavy traditional boots and seemed very dubious when I suggested they might have fewer foot problems if they wore lighter ones. My feet had given me no trouble since I'd changed the insoles in my boots back in Banff and the scars from the blisters I'd suffered from before then had now just about healed. I'd woken feeling quite pleased as I'd finally managed to seal the hole in my mattress and had had an unbroken night's sleep for the first time in a week. Early morning sunshine gave beautiful light as the damp forest steamed and mist drifted across the meadows but it didn't last and the sky was overcast within an hour.

Eight hours and eighteen miles later I arrived at Twintree Campground having seen nothing but trees, mud and rain plus two parties consisting of a lone Canadian doing the trail for the second time and a two-German/ one-Irishman trio who said they were having fun despite the weather. The site on the edge of Twintree Lake was pleasant though the half given over to horse parties was in a mess. I had a crisis during dinner when I suddenly couldn't face eating the dehydrated meal I'd cooked. 'Dump all dinners except noodles . . . I can't stand them any more!' I wrote in my journal. I knew this wasn't very practical but writing it made me feel better. If I'd known what was to happen at Grande Cache I wouldn't have worried about having to eat the meals anyway. Nor did I know that in three weeks time I would have paid a fortune for just one of those dried meals!

Shafts of sunlight illuminating the lake and the surrounding hills gave a good start to the day but again the clouds and rain closed in rapidly. The NBT forest plod was broken by the crossing of 6600-foot Snake Indian Pass, the trail's highpoint, where meadows and views opened out and the sun appeared between the showers. The yellows and reds of the vegetation around the pass showed that at this elevation summer was over and autumn well under way. For the first time I realised that I still had a long way to go and time was starting to run out. Back in the sodden forest I descended to Oatmeal Campground. As I came out of the trees into the open meadows of the site I could hear whistling. A figure appeared and looked relieved on seeing me. 'I heard you approaching and thought it was a bear,' he said, the toilet roll in his hand showing where he'd been. Stu Dechka was from Calgary and walking the whole of the NBT. Once I'd set up camp we lit a fire and huddled round it for a long and wide-ranging discussion that went from politics (Stu being a trade union activist) to conservation and the NBT itself. I was uncomplimentary about it but Stu pointed out that it depended what you wanted. He was seeing more wildlife (especially birds) and more flowers than he did on above-timberline walks and was really enjoying the trail. The weather? 'Well, it's what you expect in the mountains,' he said. I realised that I'd been spoilt by the good weather and spectacular trails earlier in the summer. I wanted the hot sunny weather and the clear skies of the Rockwall Trail all the time.

As we discussed other walks and trails Stu asked me the question that most amazed me on the whole walk.

'You're not Chris Townsend, are you?' he asked. I stared at him, unable to believe what I'd heard him say.

'How do you know?' I asked when I regained the power of speech.

'I've read your book, *The Great Backpacking Adventure*,' he replied. 'I found it in Calgary Central Library.'

This explained matters as I didn't know the book, then the only one I'd had published, was available in Canada. Even so I still thought (and still think) that the coincidence was amazing. What was also amazing, though I couldn't have known it at the time, was that Stu was the last walker I was to share a campsite with on the walk even though I was slightly less than half way.

A porcupine, unfortunately by no means the last one I was to see on the walk, woke me at 4am snuffling round the tent. Outside rain was falling. By 8.30am it had just about stopped though the sky remained dull and grey. Stu and I continued talking over a lengthy breakfast before heading off in opposite directions. To combat the rain Stu had an umbrella tied to the top of his pack with his Gore-tex jacket spread over the pack as a waterproof cover. He was travelling with a very light load but still wasn't happy with his pack which he said was very uncomfortable.

A good, fast trail down to Three Slides Campground gave a good view of glaciers on distant Upright Mountain. Two days before, John and Ann had told me how pleased they'd been to see Mount Robson earlier in the walk as that meant that even if it was in cloud when they reached Berg Lake they would have seen it. I knew from the *Trail Guide* that what they'd seen was Upright Mountain but I hadn't the heart to tell them. Looking at the distant shining peak I could see why they'd thought it was Robson. At Three Slides I met four cold, wet and miserable-looking backpackers. They were students from Wisconsin and had expected better weather so they hadn't brought much in the way of warm clothing. They only had ultralight, thin showerproof jackets and ponchos and were not enjoying themselves very much. Hoping to live off fish they caught, they hadn't brought much food either. As they hadn't caught many fish they were growing rather hungry. Despite leaving some at Berg Lake I still had too much food so I seized the opportunity to do them a favour whilst helping myself by cutting down the weight I was carrying and handed over some of my surplus supplies. What they made of wholefood mulligatawny cup-a-soups, Scottish oatcakes and dehydrated vegetable and soya meals I don't know but I imagine if they were hungry enough they'd have eaten anything. I had now met nineteen walkers in four days on the NBT. I was to meet no more for the rest of the walk.

The trail beyond Three Slides was more open than elsewhere on the NBT with views over the wide, marshy floodplain of the Snake Indian River. Clearing heavy rain produced a beautiful rainbow over Blue Creek. I took the risk of getting my camera wet and took several photographs. Blue Creek Campground lies 36 miles from the eastern end of the NBT but was the end of that trail for me. From the site I would head north up Blue Creek and then finally leave Jasper National Park for the Willmore Wilderness at Hardscrabble Pass.

Blue Creek was a spacious site which I had to myself, though like others on the NBT the section set aside for horse parties was strewn with garbage including scraps of food. I burnt what I could but it was all sodden so much was left. Apart from the unsightliness and squalor, a dirty site leads to other more serious problems as I found out the next morning. I was having breakfast under a tree, as it was raining again, when I heard a loud rustle from the bushes just twenty feet away. I looked up just as a black bear poked its face out of the foliage. I jumped up and shouted and it backed into the bushes. I could still see it so I blew my safety whistle loudly and it took off into the forest. I wasn't convinced it had gone far, though, so I packed up hastily and left. This was the only time a bear came into a campsite whilst I was there and I'm convinced it was the food scraps left by previous campers that attracted it.

A cool wind blew from the north bringing bursts of sunshine, lots of clouds and some showers. It was still the best weather for a week though, as gone were the lowering cast-iron skies and the enervating humidity. Now I had left the NBT, which, despite Stu Dechka's unanswerable defence of it, I hadn't really enjoyed, the scenery improved dramatically too. I walked up the lovely wide-open valley of Blue Creek admiring the limestone peaks of the Ancient Wall that stretched away into the distance along the east side of the valley and the lower red-coloured hills to the west. I passed at a distance a horse party setting up camp before I reached the Caribou Inn Campground. As I was coming to expect, the site had been fairly recently trashed by a horse party with much fresh cut wood and the remains of bough beds lying around. I lit a fire and huddled under the tarp as more showers blew in. This was my last night in a national park and my thoughts turned to the unknown lands to the north. After 60 days and 725 miles the 'easy' part of the walk was over.

An unpromising start with a cold north wind and low grey clouds ended up as the 'best and longest day since the Moose River' (journal entry for August 21). The spacious upper Blue Creek valley was attractive even under the drab sky. Glimmers of blue began to appear through the clouds as I climbed steeply cross-country above Azure Lake through a belt of trees into still colourful but fading alpine flower meadows and then a series of rock terraces that led to Hardscrabble Pass, an impressive doorway to the Willmore Wilderness Park. The wind on the pass was bitter. I even needed gloves. But the view was superb. All around were the slanting strata typical of Front Range peaks. As I began the descent through rocky terrain and down some big flat slabs with not a tree in sight and rock peaks and ridges all around, the sun came out and the clouds turned to white cumulus. A joyous walk down the valley of the West Sulphur River ensued with good light and good views. I shot a roll and a half of film. For the first time in weeks I felt really light-hearted and light-footed. The burden of pushing on in bad weather had gone with the returning sun.

I had a black and white 1:100,000 scale Forest Service map of the Wilderness I'd bought in Jasper townsite which showed the approximate locations of the outfitters' trails that I wanted to follow. The actual trails only bore a relation to those on the map by being in the same valley but that was enough. Eventually I reached the South Sulphur River and the first of many knee-deep fords before I arrived at an outfitter's campsite by Zenda Creek. I was out of the parks and away from permits and restrictions now. Only the nature of the terrain and the time would determine where I camped. When a good used site presented itself, though, it seemed unwise to pass it by so I stopped at this one. There was a trail sign nearby carved on a moose antler and several more moose antlers were nailed to trees at the site, one listing the members of a party who'd been here a month previously on a fishing trip. The party had consisted of ten people, nineteen horses and two dogs, the size perhaps showing why horse groups made such an impact on the land. They'd had good weather, they wrote. I was having good weather too, this being the first day it hadn't rained out of the last ten.

With clear skies the night was cold with frost rather than dampness. A temperature in the tent of +2°C was chilly enough to wake me at 2.30am and have me donning my polypro underwear. At dawn the flysheet was white with frost and I lit a fire for warmth, something that was to become the norm for the last half of the walk. The day that followed, however, was the hottest and clearest for weeks. I continued down the river valley in willow thickets and forest to emerge into the vast meadows beside the Sulphur River Cabin, a neat forest service hut left open for use by visitors. It even had a log book which I skimmed through, noting that two mountain bikers had passed through earlier in the summer and an entry from Wild Rose Outfitters complaining about the garbage others left and the need for users of the wilderness to look after it. They'd been through the area cleaning up sites recently, they wrote, which was probably why I found the campsites in far better condition than those in the northern half of Jasper National Park. A large amount of food was stored in the hut and I couldn't resist the temptation of swapping some of mine for something different. It was still dehydrated but made for a change. I also donated a couple of paperbacks I'd read to the hut shelves.

I continued on through woods above the Sulphur River intending to camp at the base of Hayden Ridge, which Rocky Notnes, when he'd described this route to me over the phone back in Jasper, had said I had to cross as the Sulphur River ran through an impassable canyon at the base of it. The tone of voice in which he mentioned the ridge suggested there was something none too pleasant about it. I was thinking it was time to look for a campsite when a short climb up a very steep abandoned fire road presented itself. I though it was just a way across a low spur so I set off up it. It went round a corner and continued climbing, which surprised me a little but I went on, sure it would drop back down to the river very soon. It didn't. It continued to climb but I'd gone too far to turn back before it occurred to me that this must be Hayden Ridge. The ascent seemed never-ending, with the trail winding back and forth so that at some point I faced every direction of the compass. Each time I thought it would level out it would twist back on itself and continue climbing. In the west the sun was setting though the evening was warm—too warm, as there was no water anywhere. Tired, thirsty and sweaty, my legs aching with the effort, I now understood the tone in Rocky Notnes' voice when he'd referred to this ridge. The top came eventually, of course, but there followed an equally long descent down to Cowlick Creek and a well-used campsite in a grove of aspens which I reached just as it was getting dark at 9.30pm. Thankfully I stopped, set up camp by torch light, lit a fire and drank three cups of coffee and ate two of the Sulphur Cabin meals without a break before climbing into the sleeping bag. I'd walked at least 25 miles and been on the trail for $11^1/2$ hours. But I was only seven or eight miles from the town of Grande Cache, my next supply point.

Three and half hours' walking through pleasant forested foothills brought me to the town and the Mountain Village Motel; $50 for two nights. Grande Cache is a small mining town, built only fifteen years earlier to service a new open cast coal mine. The post office had piles of mail: half a dozen letters, the parcel with my fleece clothing in it I'd sent from Elkford, another parcel with a new pair of boots and a new sleeping bag that John Traynor had sent from England via a person in Calgary called Sean Dougherty of whom I'd never heard but who'd included a nice letter. Conspicuously missing though was my supply box. I shrugged aside a shiver of worry and rang the Prince George post office. Most of the mail had been forwarded from there following Cia's request to them to do so. She'd sent me a note here saying they'd agreed to send stuff on. Prince George had no record of the box. We've sent on all your mail, they said, but it could still be in transit, wait a few days and see if it turns up. This was not something I wanted to hear but it was too late to do anything until the next day. I retired to the motel sunk in gloom. I could replace food and film in Grande Cache but not maps, as I'd found by a quick visit to all the likely shops. Without maps I could hardly venture into the trailless wilderness north of Willmore Park. I could only hope my supply box would turn up the next day.

Interlude Two: Grande Cache Days

24th to 30th August

The unwanted stay in Banff seemed to be repeating itself, as I hurried down to the post office on my first morning in Grande Cache to hear that my parcel had not turned up. I knew it might be lost for ever and that I'd better acquire some maps from elsewhere. The Forest Service office couldn't help with my route once I left Alberta for British Columbia, which I would do only a few days out from Grande Cache. They only carried maps for their own area. The warden merely warned me about the Muddywater River ford in the Willmore Wilderness. A backpacker had drowned there three years ago, he said.

Nowhere else in Grande Cache had anything more than road maps so I rang the nearest forestry offices in British Columbia, those at Chetwynd and Dawson Creek. Joanne at the latter was very helpful and offered to put together a package of maps for me. I rang back in the afternoon and she said the package was ready and would be sent cash on delivery by air via a private courier. I rang the couriers to check I would receive it soon, remembering the private couriers who'd transported my replacement pack to Banff. It was a Wednesday, I'd have the pack by Friday, they said. This meant another day of waiting but I felt optimistic.

By Friday I was desperate to leave. The weather had remained hot and sunny and I had run out of things to do. I'd no books to read and the television in my motel room was driving me crazy. I roamed the town from restaurant to restaurant and shop to shop buying some new socks, a pair of wool mitts for the cold weather to come, a replacement hat for the one lost on the Tonquin Creek bushwhack and an endless supply of newspapers and magazines. I also phoned the post office in Fort St. John and asked them if they would forward my supply box to Hudson Hope where, I'd discovered, there was a post office (the information I'd received from the British Columbia tourist board before the walk being that there wasn't one, which is why the box had gone to Fort St John). It would save some time not to have to travel there to pick up the box.

Friday came and no maps arrived. Neither did my supply box. I rang the couriers. Nothing to be done until Monday they said. I was forced to accept that I'd have to wait another two boring days in town, days I couldn't afford to lose in terms of time, and days I couldn't afford to pay for either. But I had no choice.

With nothing else to do I joined the local library over the weekend! This was a first on a long distance walk! They had a number of books on mountaineering in the Rockies and on the Willmore Wilderness which I read avidly. Monday arrived and still no maps. I increased my phone bill by more calls to the couriers. They couldn't trace the package. I couldn't believe it. Tuesday came and went and again no parcel but by the end of the day I'd rung several of the courier offices along the route and had finally located the parcel in the town of Edmonton where I suspected it had been since Friday. It would, I was promised, be with me the next day. The supply box still hadn't turned up either. Accepting that it was lost for good I replaced the missing supplies at the local supermarket, buying what seemed to be equivalent items to those in the vanished supply box. I'd now been in Grande Cache a week which, given the age of the town, made me feel like a resident.

The real residents had noticed this permanent guest as well and Alex Didow, the owner of the shop where I bought my daily paper, finally asked me what I was doing. He then introduced me to Marc Salesse, a photographer and wilderness enthusiast from Quebec who had settled in Grande Cache and who offered to take me canoeing, another first on a long distance walk!

That afternoon saw Marc wrestling a Canadian-style open canoe down a steep bank into the Sulphur River canyon whilst I watched. He then gave me a brief lesson in paddling techniques, stuck me in the front of the vessel and pushed off. Never having been in a canoe before I found the ten-mile voyage very exciting, especially as it involved running some grade two and grade three rapids, small scale stuff to the experienced I'm sure, but quite an adventure for me. The canyon was impressive and, as Marc pointed out, could only be seen from a canoe as the great rock walls on either side soared straight up from the water. We stopped to explore a few caves and, after I'd been a bit slow in following commands, to bale out the canoe. Eventually we came to the rock pillars of Sulphur Gates and the much enlarged Smoky River, which I'd last seen as a small creek far away on the North Boundary Trail. Mark took us into what he described as the vortex on the Smoky where conflicting currents in the water held the canoe in place. The surging waters under the canoe felt incredibly powerful and I was quite relieved when we paddled out of the vortex and down the wide, choppy river to beach at a roadhead. Marc was intending to undertake a long solo canoe trip down the Smoky to its confluence with the Peace River in the autumn. He canoed in the summer and skied with a sledge in the winter, he told me, because in both cases he could transport heavy loads much more easily than on his back in a rucksack. My method of travel was not for him. He'd settled here because it was out of the busy mainstream of the national parks but still offered superb protected wilderness mountains.

On the last day of August, eight days after arriving in Grande Cache, the Forest Service maps finally arrived. I dashed back to my motel room and opened the bundle. Some muddy almost incomprehensible blow-ups of aerial photographs tumbled out along with a blue and white 1:250,000 map. Joanne had added various roads and route suggestions in red ink onto the map. In the bottom corner she'd written 'the southern roads on this map are very approximate locations—refer to air photos.' Fine, except that I couldn't relate the air photos to the map. 'Should be fun for 250 miles,' I wrote in my journal.

I decided I was going anyway, despite the poor nature of the maps. Why, I asked myself, had I relied on others? If I'd hitch-hiked or caught a bus to Edmonton, the nearest big city where maps would be available, I might have been away for a couple of days but I'd have had better maps and I'd have been on the trail again by now. The reason of course was the private courier company. If they'd said it would take a week for the maps to reach me, I would have gone to get them myself. As it was always 'tomorrow', I'd waited. But now finally I could continue the walk.

Lost in the Foothills

Grande Cache to Redwillow Creek
31st August to 13th September   242 miles

Before I could leave I had to sort out a route on my new map, a route that bore little resemblance to my original one that assumed the use of 1:50,000 topo maps and that stayed close to the crest of the range. My new route based on Joanne Smith of the Dawson Creek Forest Service's suggestions went back into the Willmore Wilderness and west to the Divide, but then made a large loop into the foothills to the east along logging roads before returning to below the Divide at Monkman Provincial Park. From there a section of cross-country travel led to the Sakunka Forest Road which in turn led to the town of Chetwynd, my intended next supply point, though my next supply box was another two days' walk further on in Hudson Hope. So much for the theory. I had grave doubts about being able to follow this route in practice. Apart from the approximate positioning of the southern roads there were some cross-country sections that I knew would be very difficult if not impossible to navigate across in bad weather using a small scale blue and white map with little detail on it.

Initially the good weather of the past week continued and I left Grande Cache at 2.30pm in high spirits after being treated to lunch by Alex Didow. A local reporter joined me before I left the road to interview me for his paper. Then I was off past Sulphur Gates and along the Smoky River on a good outfitter's trail for fifteen miles before camping in a large meadow. The night was windy but warm (11°C) and in my new sleeping bag I was too hot. It was with relief that I peered out of the tent to see the pale dawn light on the woods and hills instead of waking to the sight of a blank motel wall as I had for the last week. Still in the Willmore Wilderness I had a good trail to follow all day and good views over the Smoky and Muddywater Rivers. The ford of the latter was knee-deep but certainly not dangerous after ten days of dry weather. A large horse party passed me here, reminding me that the hunting season was beginning.

Camp was by a large duck-inhabited pond in deep, closed-in Dry Canyon. That evening I did some route calculations and realised I was three weeks behind schedule and would probably not finish before mid-October. When would the first snows come? I slept badly that night, constantly waking with thoughts of the route on my mind.

Perhaps my disturbed sleep explains what occurred the next day when I walked 20 miles but only progressed 12. It started well enough along the continuing good trail down Dry Canyon and across Sheep Creek to the Famm Creek valley. There was a trail here too, but it criss-crossed the creek constantly so my feet were permanently wet. Two rather dishevelled, not to say disreputable-looking, horse riders with eight pack horses came towards me (and I wonder just how I looked after weeks in the wilderness?). They said I should have stayed by Sheep Creek which was a better and faster route than Famm Creek for anyone on foot and they gave me some suggestions for the route to come. I was becoming fed up with the constant creek fords and the chest-deep willow thickets I was thrashing through and looking up at the green treeless ridges above I wondered if a route along them would be easier. It would certainly provide good views. Whilst my mind was musing on a high-level route I took a wrong turning and happily followed a trail up the wrong valley for over four miles and a thousand feet of ascent until I reached a pass that shouldn't have been there. My mind was not on navigation for I'd already fleetingly noticed that the sun was to my right not to my left where it should have been yet the significance of this had not registered. As I was still on the Willmore Wilderness map I could see what I'd done but I felt very chastened as I retraced my steps and continued up the right valley to an outfitter's campsite.

My journal entry for the next day begins: 'Hm. Now I know what cross-country is like!' On reaching the divide between Famm and Trench Creeks I'd been tempted by the sunny, open slopes above and had scrambled up a steep loose gully to the ridge above and an unnamed 7300-foot peak which gave great views across the winding green ridges of the Willmore hills to the snowy flanks of Mount Sir Alexander and Mount Vreeland away to the west. I was aiming to cut a corner and descend to another valley, Cote Creek, where I could pick up another outfitter's trail. I worked out a route from my vantage point and then set off on a glorious high-level ridge walk round the head of Narrow Creek to a col below another unnamed peak. A coyote ambled past me at a distance of only twenty feet on the col with barely a glance in my direction. The descent to Cote Creek was a complex one through thick forest and around small crags on a steep hillside. Once I reached the creek I camped. It had been a wonderful day, hot and clear again, but I'd only walked 12 miles, hence my journal comments.

The perfect weather seemed to belong to the Willmore Wilderness, having begun at Hardscrabble Pass and with a flicker of rain and a touch of grey skies starting to break at the col at the head of Cote Creek that marked my departure from the park. The trail up the creek had been sketchy, and willow bashing and endless fords had been the order of the day until I found an old, disused cut line shortly before the col. Cut lines are made by mining companies when they prospect for oil or coal. They simply hack a dead straight line through the forest that may run for miles and do some test sampling along it. Although usually overgrown these lines often provide easier walking than the forest either side and I was to use many of them during the second half of the walk. The line led me down to Cecilia Creek then stopped. I cast around for the trail that was meant to follow the creek but couldn't find it so had to resort to some desperate struggles for a couple of hours through the dense willow thickets until I reached an old overgrown logging road with a recently cleared trail cut down the middle of it. Beside the start of the road was a cleared area in the forest with a large fire circle in the middle of it. I had seen nowhere for hours where I could have made a comfortable camp, so I stopped and set up the tent. I checked the map and saw I wasn't far from the dirt road leading to Kakwa Lake which I wanted to reach. I didn't appreciate at the time just how nice it was to know where I was. I noted in my journal that I hoped to be in Hudson's Hope in eleven days, little thinking it would take me twenty-four.

The old track led to the Kakwa River, an easy ford and the road, which took me to an area signposted as the Wild Kakwa Wild Land Recreation Area which I'd not heard of before. I was now embarked on the most problematic part of my route for I was not on any map I was carrying at all but had to work my way in a loop east, north and then west to get back on my 1:250,000 map and hopefully hit the logging road beside Huguenot Creek. The diversion was necessary to bypass some steep, thickly-wooded hills that lay between me and the road. In retrospect I'd have been better fighting my way across those hills, however tough it might have been, and staying on the map. But it's easy to say now what I should have done. A wide trail led into the recreation area with wooden bridges across the creeks. It wasn't designed for walkers though, as I found when two noisy, bulbous-tyred little four-wheeled vehicles came up behind me. I was to find these all-terrain vehicles (ATVs), which looked to me like mini-farm tractors, a common form of transport in the northern Rockies. One of the drivers stopped for a chat and told me there were many people at Kakwa Lake where he'd been fishing as it was Labor Day, a Canadian public holiday. Most people were from the nearest town, Grande Prairie. I was given some useful advice about my route for the next few days which I was to wish I'd listened to more carefully. Down at the roadhead where they'd left their truck I met the ATVers again plus many other people including a bunch of mountain bikers. I was pointed in the right direction and told of a camp site just off the logging road I was to follow. As was becoming my habit, I spent the evening doing further route calculations, though as I noted in my journal this was the 'first night when I don't know exactly where I am'.

The journal entry ended with the words: 'Oh well. See what tomorrow brings'. The next day's journal starts: 'And it brought too much! An eleven-hour day mostly spent not knowing where I was in a storm'. What I had feared had happened. The weather had broken. I'd set off down the road looking for a turn-off to the left I'd been advised to take. Finding one I walked up it onto a high above-timberline ridge where I followed the track as it twisted and turned for an hour in a storm until it came to a dead end on the edge of a steep drop-off. The visibility was minimal with swirling cloud all around and the bitter wind and heavy rain was making me feel quite cold so I bushwhacked down through dense forest to the valley below. Here I found a trail which I followed downstream to an old cut line and then a huge cleared area, the site of an old sawmill that the ATVers had told me to look out for. I set off in a westward direction along a wide cut line I'd been recommended to follow, intending to camp by the next water as it was 6.30 pm. No water turned up and the cut line deadended, leaving me to follow bits of game trails down to what I thought was Saxon Creek, arriving at 9pm with just enough time to set up camp before it grew dark. Vehicle lights across the wide creek told me there must be a road there.

A strong wind blew all night, though by dawn the skies had cleared. The trail led to a ford and an outfitter's camp with several vehicles but no people. A road and then trails and cut lines led me north for hours until I found myself on a bluff high above a steep-sided river gorge. I reached the river via a tricky descent and then had a wide, crutch-deep ford in milky fast-flowing water over slippery boulders which was more difficult than I'd thought it would be. I was very relieved to reach the far shore even though I then had to climb a steep bank to avoid more sheer cliffs. Further along I dropped back down to the river again and camped on the edge of some large shingle banks where I lit a big driftwood fire and tried to work out which river this was. I guessed at the Narraway but had to concede that it was no more than a guess. My supplies were dwindling too. In Grande Cache Marc had persuaded me to buy a length of fishing line and a few weights and hooks in case I ran out of food so I dug these out of the pack and put out a two-hook night line baited with raisins and cooked noodles.

92

As for the route, all I knew was that I needed to head north-west so that was the direction I would go in. At this point I was frustrated rather than worried, feeling I couldn't be far from where I wanted to be. I was in a region of low, densely-forested hills and deep river canyons, the foothills of the Rockies. This is where I should have been, but unfortunately the nature of the terrain made navigation very difficult as there were no treeless hilltops from which an overview of the area could be obtained and compass bearings taken. Of course this would have been the case even if I'd had the proper maps.

At dawn my boots were frozen solid and there was a heavy frost. My night line came in empty which didn't surprise me. I was to use it several more times in the days to come with the same success. A day of bushwhacking through dense vegetation, broken only by short stretches of cut line, left me at a very similar riverbank campsite, this time amongst beaver-gnawed aspens. It could have been the same river. I wasn't sure. The day had been cold and cloudy with heavy rain in the afternoon that gave way to a pink sunset and a clear night sky. I sat by my fire counting out my supplies. I had 2½ days' food left. The first twitches of worry came into my mind. How lost could I be? I tried to avoid that emotive, potentially panic-inducing word fraught with unpleasant implications. I wasn't lost, I told myself, just unsure of my whereabouts, a state I was to remain in for the next week.

Rain fell at 4.30pm, the wet tent was frozen by dawn. A thick river mist slowly cleared as the sun rose, blood-red, over the forest. Most of the day was spent engaged in a desperate bushwhack through boggy spruce forest. I only found three cut lines and these all deadended after a short distance. I also had to cross three deep creek canyons, one of which I had to follow south-west before I could find a way down into it and up the far bank. It was a tiring way to travel. Bushwhacking isn't really an adequate description for how I progressed but it's better than walking which hardly gives the flavour of the slithering, slipping, sliding descents in the canyons and the strenuous thrash through jungles of alder and willow in the forest, made worse all too often by the presence of muskeg: deep moss-covered slimy swamplands that virtually stopped all progress. I finished the day by descending to the nearest river to camp and choosing the worst spot to do so: a steep, loose bank of tangled vegetation that ended in a sheer drop above the water, forcing me to thrash along the bank for a while until I could scramble down onto some shingle banks. However a highlight on an otherwise depressing day was my first sight of a beaver which slid down the bank in front of me then swam away upstream. I hoped that the river wasn't the same one I'd left that morning but again I wasn't sure. Huddled under my tarp I discovered to my annoyance that I'd lost my binoculars and some camera lens filters. My bumbag zip must have become opened without my realising it in the dense bushes. The constant fight with the undergrowth was taking its toll on my clothes too, with my trousers suffering a ripped ankle and a torn crutch. It had been another day of little apparent progress. In the words of my journal: 'not a good day'.

By now I was stifling growing feelings of worry and simply going on in a roughly northerly direction. All thoughts of finding the right track had vanished. My aim now was to hit the east-west running gravel highway that lay to the north and then hitch-hike into the town of Tumbler Ridge and buy some food. A damp, cool morning had me setting off clad in my waterproofs as the bushes were sodden. What was now the daily pattern followed as I bushwhacked through dense forest in an area of deep canyons with steep, loose sides which were very difficult to cross, often forcing me to turn east and even south to find ways over them. There were at least three areas on the map where I could be, none of them where I wanted to be. I started rationing my food, having just a packet of soup for lunch. I had been feeling hungry for the last few days. The feeling was to grow. Part of the reason was that the replacement supplies I'd bought in Grande Cache were not proving as sustaining as the more carefully planned supplies that had gone astray. The day ended high on the rim of a canyon where I camped, as with night falling and no clear way down it seemed unwise to try a descent. There were no creeks nearby and I hadn't seen any for hours, but luckily I had filled my litre bottle at a creek earlier in the day and so had a little water. I now had just one day's food left and despite walking hard for eleven hours with barely a halt, still had no idea where I was.

My biggest worry was not losing my physical strength, despite the energy-sapping bushwhacking and the dwindling of my supplies, as I knew that even without food I could probably keep going for a week or more as long as I had water. Mental determination was what I must maintain. I had to suppress all feelings of panic or hopelessness and simply plug grimly onwards trying to convince myself that over the next hill, across the next river I would find a track or trail. I then had to stop myself from feeling too disappointed when over and over again I was faced with more forest and another river canyon. Through this section I walked with my mind locked on the immediate details of finding a route through the jungle in front of me. I rarely stopped for a break. There seemed no point. This meant that each evening I was so exhausted I had no time to sit and worry.

A breakfast of crackers spread with margarine and half a cup of coffee was not to my stomach's liking and repeated on me all day, leaving a greasy film in my mouth. It took me an hour and a half to scramble down to the creek where I had a second breakfast identical to the first except that the coffee cup was full. The usual tiring bushwhack led to a much bigger river than any of the others which, when I eventually managed to clamber down to it, I crossed where it split into four channels, each one knee deep. On the far bank I found some fresh boot prints which made me feel ridiculously like Robinson Crusoe. I had begun to think I was far from other people and in an area no-one ever visited. I climbed up the steep slopes above the river to find a series of cut lines which I followed northwards past a long-abandoned horse wagon overgrown with grass and other plants. Suddenly I could see a dark line ahead. I hurried on to find a dirt road. I was delighted enough to take a photograph of it. I followed it for maybe six miles in a north-easterly direction passing a marker saying 'Alberta Survey Marker - Do Not Remove'. Alberta? I should have been well into British Columbia by now. If I was still in Alberta I must have been travelling north but not west since I left the Kakwa River. I took a side track west from the road after it deadended at a drilling rig and then a cut line as far as a beaver pond which lay across the track. I camped here as I was very thirsty, having come across no water for several hours, and anyway it was nearly dark and I'd been walking for twelve hours.

As I set up camp a beaver began swimming around the pond thrashing the water with a loud crack with its tail when it dived. I watched enthralled for several minutes until I was distracted by a magnificent sunset, the best of the walk so far, which was reflected in the pond. Hunger and worries over being lost forgotten, I set up the tripod and took a series of photographs. Then I ate my last dried food, a packet of noodles, normally only part of my evening meal. I laid out my remaining supplies: a quarter packet of crackers, a half packet of onion soup, a full packet of vegetable soup plus a handful of granola, two teaspoons of coffee, one teaspoon of sugar, a few dates, a little dried milk and some calorie-free coffee sweeteners. As I noted in my journal: 'it sounds a lot written down!' I also wrote: 'I have an inkling of where I am and what I've been doing the last five days. If I'm where I think I am, the river I forded was the Wapiti, and I could be only 12 miles from the road network to Tumbler Ridge. I hope I find out tomorrow.' Tomorrow was September 13th. The day after was my birthday.

Studying the map, I worked out I was in the foothills forty or fifty miles north and west of where I wanted to be. How I'd arrived here I wasn't sure except that I must have not gone as far west as I'd thought. My position was confirmed the next morning when cut lines led me to Alberta/British Columbia boundary marker number 68.2. The marker positions were shown on my map so for the first time for eight days I knew exactly where I was. Not far north lay the gravel highway running between Grande

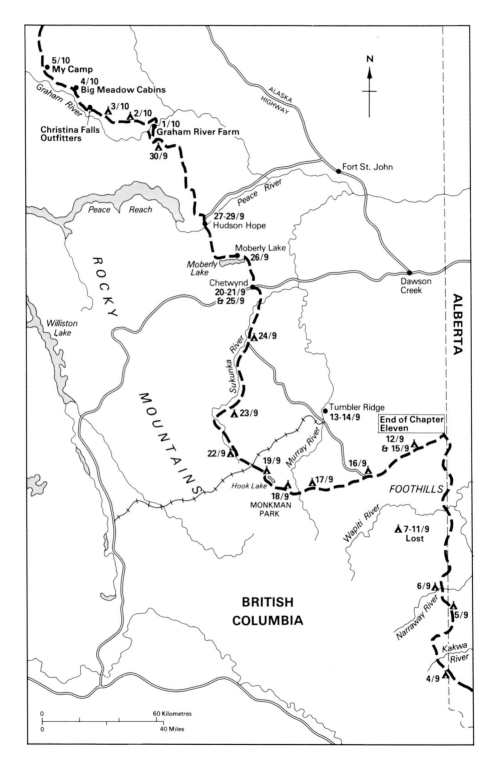

5/10
My Camp

4/10
Big Meadow Cabins

3/10

2/10

Graham River

Christina Falls
Outfitters

1/10
Graham River Farm

30/9

ALASKA HIGHWAY

Fort St. John

Peace River

Peace Reach

27-29/9
Hudson Hope

Moberly Lake
26/9

Moberly
Lake

Chetwynd
20-21/9
& 25/9

Dawson
Creek

ALBERTA

R O C K Y

Williston
Lake

Sukunka River

24/9

23/9

22/9

Tumbler Ridge
13-14/9

End of Chapter
Eleven
12/9
& 15/9

M O U N T A I N S

19/9

Murray River

16/9

Hook Lake

18/9
MONKMAN
PARK

17/9

FOOTHILLS

Wapiti River

7-11/9
Lost

BRITISH
COLUMBIA

6/9

Narraway River

5/9

Kakwa
River

4/9

N

| 0 | | 60 Kilometres |
| 0 | | 40 Miles |

Prairie and Tumbler Ridge according to the map. Several hours of cut lines later and I reached a dirt road. A pick-up truck was heading towards me. I flagged it down and had my first conversation with anyone other than myself in eight days. The driver was heading the wrong way, towards Grande Prairie, but he was able to tell me exactly where I was. He looked at my map and laughed. 'This road has been closed for years,' he said, 'and is only used by oil company vehicles like mine. However in twelve miles you'll reach Redwillow Creek and the new Heritage Highway which goes to Tumbler Ridge.' I debated taking a lift to Grande Prairie but decided the situation wasn't that desperate. I could manage twelve miles on a road. It was now 4.15pm so I drank the last of my soup and coffee and set off. I felt both relieved at knowing I was out of the wilderness and angry at what seemed to have been a highly incompetent performance. How could I hope to get through the much vaster, wilder areas still to come? I became depressed about the chances of finishing the walk as my mind went round in circles of self-recrimination until I realised I had to think about something else. I had obligations, I told myself, sponsors to satisfy, lectures to give, a book to write. How could I face John Traynor if I didn't finish the walk? Slowly I wrenched my mind away from thoughts of failure. How would I write the book? I made myself run through a detailed plan with chapter titles and contents. Ideas began to come to the surface, the first inspiration of any sort I'd had in a week, so closed had my mind been to any thoughts about my situation. It had been better not to think. The book plan pleased me (I wish I could remember it now!) and my mood changed to one of optimism.

About four miles from the highway I heard a pick-up behind me. I stuck out my thumb and got a lift to the highway with two hunters who were going to Grande Prairie. They didn't think much of my chances of getting a lift to Tumbler Ridge that night. By the highway was a campground with a pick-up with a camper unit attached and a car parked in front of the picnic tables. I sat down and waited for the traffic. The car from the campground pulled out and passed me. It was full. A road sign told me it was forty-eight miles to Tumbler Ridge. I could walk it if I had to but not today. No other traffic came, so at 8.30 I wandered over to the campground and pitched the tent. The camper was in darkness with no people around, though the embers of a campfire glowed in the darkness nearby.

Just as I was setting up the stove on a picnic table by the light of my headlamp, I heard the sound of high-pitched engines. I looked up to see two ATVs pull up by the camper. I waited until a light came on and then wandered down to their site. Two men were standing by the camper. I felt very nervous. It was late in the evening, miles from anywhere and I imagined that after two weeks in the wilderness I must look pretty rough. I had rehearsed my lines. I said:

'Do you have any food you can sell me?' having decided this was the best approach. There was silence as the two men stared at me. Finally one of them spoke:

'Where the hell have you come from?'

I explained. As I did so one of the men started bringing items out of the camper and putting them on the picnic table where a large camping grill was set up. I was handed a can of Pepsi-Cola. It tasted ridiculously wonderful. My hosts introduced themselves as Rick Foster and Bruce Dyer from Tumbler Ridge where they worked as miners, though originally they were from Saskatchewan and Newfoundland respectively. No-one was from Tumbler Ridge, it being a new company mining town created just a few years previously. This was an evening off and they'd come out on a moose hunt.

Rick apologised for their initially cool reaction to me. 'We saw your light but no vehicle when we came back and wondered what you were doing here,' he explained. I realised that to be without a vehicle this far from anywhere was rather suspicious, added to which my appearance didn't help. Once they'd satisfied themselves that I was genuine and not a fugitive from justice they couldn't have been more friendly. Without mentioning it, Rick had begun to prepare a meal for me of fresh salad, foil-baked potatoes and grilled steak.

'How do you like your steak?' he asked. Bruce answered for me: 'Anyway it comes. He'd eat it raw!' He was quite right. I devoured the meal as Rick and Bruce broke open some cans of beer and Bruce put on a cassette tape of Newfoundland music which sounded like Irish showband tunes to me and reminisced about his home province. Every so often he wandered down to the creek to bring back some driftwood for the now blazing fire. Fascinated by my Petzl headlamp, the like of which he'd never seen before, he borrowed it and came back with his arms full of wood, raving about how great it was. I promised to send him and Rick one each when I returned home.

We talked on into the night as more beer was opened and Rick produced a bottle of home-made liqueur to drink as well. I talked about my journey, the euphoria of having been 'rescued' by the two of them, overwhelming feelings of tiredness induced by the alcohol, and my twelve-hour twenty-five-plus-mile day, not to mention the restricted diet and over-exertion of previous days. Bruce couldn't believe that anyone would walk about alone and unarmed in the mountains. 'What about the grizzlies?' he asked. I couldn't explain it, I just felt safe, I said. The night becoming colder we retreated into the camper for coffee and more liqueurs. At 5pm I finally crawled into my sleeping bag.

Feeling surprisingly refreshed I sat in the hot sun with Rick and Bruce the next day over a lengthy breakfast that turned into lunch before they drove back to Tumbler Ridge where I checked into the only motel. That evening I sat down with my maps and did some careful planning. I knew from the last week that I couldn't bushwhack my way to the end of the Rockies. Also I was entering a fairly developed area of the mountains with many logging areas, plus coal mines, gas plants, rail lines and more. Looking at the map I could see that, apart from a short section around Hook Lake, I could walk dirt roads most of the way to Hudson Hope whilst staying in the mountains. I had no choice but to adopt this route. North of Hudson Hope I would have to go cross-country as there were no roads. If it was like the area south of here I doubted whether I could finish the walk.

I spent my 39th birthday eating. Despite the urgent need to press on I felt I had to have a couple of days to recover from the last fortnight, so I spent an extra day in Tumbler Ridge. One potentially major problem did occur when the bank only let me withdraw a small amount on my VISA card. 'You're over your limit,' they said. I knew I'd spent much more than intended in Grande Cache so I was hardly surprised. I needed more funds however to buy food for the next section, so I rang John Traynor in England for assistance. After all he was my base camp manager! Organised and efficient as ever, he told me not to worry, he'd sort it out. I gave him time to do so then rang again to be told he'd telexed £85 to me and paid money into my account. I'd worry about the actual state of my finances when I returned home; for the moment I was just glad to have some cash. The missing supply box was costing far more than it was worth, I thought, as I stocked up with more food. Back at the motel I rang the Hudson Hope post office to check that my supply box had been forwarded from Fort St John as I'd requested. 'Oh yes, you've lots of mail and two large parcels,' said the post mistress. Two large parcels? It sounded as though my missing box had finally turned up. I'd left Hudson Hope as a forwarding address in Grande Cache. I was going to have more than enough food for the last part of the walk. Tumbler Ridge was even newer and smaller than Grande Cache but had much the same shops and facilities and a much better choice of books. I was delighted to find a new Saul Bellow novel.

I had a birthday drink with Rick who then took me back to his house so I could use his washing machine. He'd offered me floor space but I wanted somewhere I could sort out all my gear, do some repairs and spread out my maps as well as unwind and relax, which is why I'd gone to the motel. Only as I sat in the bland motel room on the evening of my birthday did what had just happened really sink in. The abrupt jump from being alone, lost and hungry in the wilderness to a party atmosphere with Rick and Bruce had left me feeling dazed and bewildered as well as relieved. Now as I reflected on the last week I realised just how lucky I'd been. A few more days of bushwhacking could have left me unable to go on. An injury in one of the canyons could have been fatal, no-one having the faintest idea where I was. Also, walking out of the bush on the one evening when Bruce and Rick were there was quite a coincidence in itself. By the time I'd thought all this through I felt very relieved and cheerful but also aware that I had to be more careful for the rest of the journey. I couldn't afford to be lost for another week.

Roads and Helicopters

Redwillow Creek to Hudson Hope
15th to 28th September   188 miles

After a final huge meal I took a taxi back out to the Redwillow Creek Campground. It cost $92 but I felt I had to return to the walk as fast as possible. I didn't want to leave the route broken though, so after setting up camp I jogged back along the dirt road to where I'd had my first lift. The place was easy enough to identify as my boot prints were still clear in the roadside dust. I felt pleased. The journey was again unbroken. 'Tomorrow off down road on start of big push to finish,' reads my journal.

How big a push it might have to be was brought home to me the next morning. I woke to darkness and a rather slack-seeming tent. I sat up, brushing against the walls. A soft, slithering sound resulted in sudden daylight. It seemed ominously familar, and sure enough on sticking my head out of the tent I found snow falling—heavy, wet snow that already lay several inches deep on the ground. Summer was ending.

The snow had stopped falling by the time I set off and I read my way along the road on a cool, overcast day to the Stony Lake Recreation Site where I camped. A temperature of just +3°C had me lighting a fire. Dark clouds threatened more snow so I erected the tarp over a picnic table. Just as it grew dark a campavan pulled up with a canoe on the roof and a trailer loaded with an all-terrain vehicle behind. The single occupant leapt out and set off into the darkness on the ATV to return soon afterwards with a load of wood. The shrill whine of a chain saw and the dull clunk of an axe showed that here was a man prepared for all the wilderness could throw at him. At 8.30 a colder, drier snow began to fall.

By dawn the sky was clear and cold, minus 2°C at 8am. The tent and tarp were both frozen solid and a golden sun was just starting to filter through the trees. Sensing a superb sunrise I leapt up, grabbed the camera and tripod and ran down to the lakeshore. A searingly bright thin shaft of gold light pierced the thick mist that covered the water from the still tree-hidden sun. Slowly the greyness dispersed in the strengthening light, the last remnants of it twisting and swirling over the still waters in which the low distant hills could now be seen reflected. A brilliant blue sky came into view overhead. I wandered the shoreline for the half hour this special light lasted, taking many photographs. It was the most marvellous dawn on the whole walk.

Again I read most of the day as I headed back westwards into the mountains along the Kinuseo Falls road with the beautiful fall colours of aspen woods on either side. The fast approaching peaks, I noted, were snow-capped. Several four-wheel drive trucks passed, heading for the Falls, a local beauty spot on the edge of Monkman Provincial Park.

One vehicle stopped, its occupants, themselves backpackers, wanting to know what I was doing. They were a bit surprised when they found out! I stopped about six miles from the falls just before a deep and cold-looking unbridged Kinuseo Creek after a twenty-two mile day. Deciding I'd rather face the ford first thing in the morning I set up camp on the well-used but clean site on the near bank. As would happen often during the last six weeks of the walk I'd started and ended the day swathed in warm clothing but had stripped down to shorts and tee-shirt for the middle four or five hours. By 8pm the temperature was zero. By nine it was minus 4°C and I was sitting in front of a warm fire which I'd lit in a blackened fire ring. A metal grill was propped up against a tree. I used this as a support for my pans and cooked over the fire, saving a little stove fuel.

The coldest night yet ensued. At 7am it was minus 3°C inside the tent and condensation had formed and frozen on the inner tent. The outside of my sleeping bag was damp. A heavy white frost coated the long grass along the river bank. I lit a fire as soon as I was up, something I would do most mornings from now on. The tent was still frozen when I packed it away at 9.30am, the sun having only just appeared. I couldn't wait for it to thaw and dry out though. I needed every minute of daylight for walking. The knee-deep creek was edged with ice that I had to break through, a chilly start to the day's walk.

Several pick-ups that had passed me going in to the falls the day before passed me again on their way back out. Several, curious about me, stopped to talk. One couple, Mac and Gail McPherson from Fort St. John, now the nearest large town, were very interested in my walk, being keen hikers themselves. They loaded me up with some of their spare food including processed cheese slices and tins of sardines and salmon. My recent days on short rations being well-remembered I wasn't going to turn down any offers of food.

Somehow I managed to miss the falls themselves which lay off to the side of the road. By the time I found the road bridge across the Murray

River I was well past them and not about to retrace my steps. A vast open space marked the site of an old lumber mill and my departure from the road and return to the wilderness. A couple of pick-ups pulled up here, the drivers asking me where the falls were. I was not the only one to pass them by. To the west lay the main crest of the Rockies, a gently undulating, though steep-sided snow-speckled ridge here, which I would parallel as I turned northwards again.

Cold and deep fords of Imperial and Hook Creeks separated the easy walking along the road from desperate bushwhacking through thick, wet undergrowth in the Hook Creek valley. Suddenly my confident four-mile-an-hour stride collapsed into an uncoordinated stagger. After a half mile or so of this I donned my trainers, sodden anyway from the earlier fords, and followed Hook Creek itself, either in the water or, where possible, on shingle banks. I had about thirty-five miles to go to the next roadhead, all in the same valley, so I could hardly lose myself again. It was more a question of how long it would take to battle through the jungle. By late afternoon thick clouds built up in the sky and it grew very dark. I set up camp on a pebble bank, spreading the tarp over some washed-up logs in preparation for the storm I was sure would come, The temperature was much higher, 6°C at 8pm. The site was cosy with fine mountain scenery all around. I lit a fire, though I didn't really need one.

The storm began warm with rain but by 7am had cooled, to bring sleet and snow backed by a gusty wind. My camp was just below the freezing level as the snow was not settling on it though I could see the mountain slopes whitening not far above the valley. After two hours beside and often in Hook Creek I picked up an old blazed trail which I followed high up on the west side of the valley into an area of steeply sloping meadows and fir groves. The meadows were not easy to cross though, the faint line of the trail being overhung with head-high nettles and the extremely nasty poison-spined devil's club. I thrashed these aside with my stick as I climbed higher to fine views of the mountains as the clouds rose and faded away.

The increasingly difficult-to-trace trail finally vanished on the edge of a large burned area through which I had to bushwhack down to the aptly named Hook Lake which I could see shining in the forest below, a long, narrow body of water named after the curved section at the north end that was separated from the main body of the lake by a hilly, wooded promontory. I arrived by the lake at the south end of the hook itself to find a campsite, recently used by someone unconcerned about the area as they had left a mass of garbage including fishing lines, a pair of gloves and a torn training shoe. Fresh grizzly prints in the wet sand showed the mess had attracted the local bears so, although it was 5pm and I'd had a hard day, I decided I'd better find somewhere else to camp.

Across the lake I could see flat ground by the inlet stream, also called Hook Creek, no more than a mile and a half away. Between me and that potential camp site, though, lay a shoreline of steep, loose shaly bluffs and tangled deadfall backed by many small hills cut deeply into by side streams and covered with dense undergrowth and fallen burned timber: a nightmare terrain that took me over two hours to cross. I had to climb high above the little cliffs then slither cautiously back down to the lakeshore, trying not to lose control on the sliding slopes. A couple of times, though, I lost my footing and shot away down the slopes, to stop in a flurry of earth and leaves in a bush or a tangled mass of fallen tree branches. Staying upright wasn't helped by the fact that I was wearing plastic bags over my socks to try and keep my feet warm if not dry during all the creek fords which made my feet slide around in my shoes. These falls scared me. This was not the place to have an accident. Apart from the remoteness I was uncomfortably aware that there was a large number of grizzlies around. Berry bushes grew thickly on the burnt hillsides and the huge piles of purple bear dung that were scattered everywhere showed that many grizzlies were here enjoying one of their favourite late summer and fall foods. With many tracks around as well I came across far more bear sign here than in any other place on the walk. The popularity of the area with bears was to be confirmed later by local people who were very surprised I'd come through the area without meeting several grizzlies. I was worried the bears would think I was competing for their berries. Visibility was limited but I was certainly making a great deal of noise as I crashed through the undergrowth. Just to confirm my presence I let off blasts on my safety whistle at intervals too.

Finally I reached the north end of the hook where I could see that the lake was very shallow for twenty or more feet out from the bank. Tired of the bushwhacking I waded out into the silt-bottomed water and splodged my way to the inlet creek, arriving there in near-darkness to find more garbage including the remains of a large polythene, string and pole shelter on the beach. However a nice site revealed itself tucked away in a small grove of trees on the edge of the wide shore with a fire ring, grill and a long seat cut out of a fallen tree trunk. There was no rubbish here either, though I did discover a large tin of 'Frontier Stew' under the log-bench. As I'd got to it before the bears, I ate it. Although all the litter, most of it clearly left by anglers, was depressing I did gain a glimmer of optimism from it which was that it should mean there was some form of a trail for the remaining ten miles to the Sakunka River Forest Road.

I'd worn waterproofs all day but still felt chilled as soon as I stopped so I lit a large fire. Come dawn and I relit it, as again there was a hard frost with a cold, damp mist drifting off the lake. Soon after I set off I came across a crude trail hacked through the undergrowth. Its width and the many tyre tracks showed that it was designed for ATVs. I followed it on its twisting course through the forest until I lost it on the edge of a vast beaver pond. (I was, amazingly, to meet one of the makers of this trail in an outfitter's camp in a few weeks' time who told me that they'd driven straight across the beaver dam.) Unable to locate the trail I plunged into the ice-covered knee-deep water. The next few hours were some of the most unpleasant of the walk as I waded through icy beaver swamps, my feet painfully cold, probing ahead with my stick so I could avoid the deeper pools. Slowly I made my way up the valley until I finally found the branch rail line that takes coal from Tumbler Ridge to the main east-west railway. I knew then I was not far from the roadhead and indeed was there in just a few more minutes. As I stumbled out of the forest near the mouth of the tunnel that takes the railway through the mountains I was greeted by the sight of a group of people standing round two helicopters.

I wandered towards them, uncomfortably aware that everyone was staring at me.

'Where the hell have you come from?'

This was to become the standard greeting whenever I walked out of the woods from now on. I explained, and then asked a few question of my own.

'What are you doing here?' I asked them.

'We're collecting fir cones.'

'By helicopter?'

'By helicopter.'

One of the pilots explained. They flew the helicopter just above the treetops dangling a whirling blade and a basket beneath them. The first was used to lop the top ten or so feet of the tree off which then fell into the second. Yes, they said, it was dangerous, the concentration required being so great that no-one flew for more than an hour at a time, which was why they had two helicopters. Due to the gusty winds they'd stopped work for the day. Once on the ground the treetops were stripped of their cones which were wanted for the seed. A large group of local Indians were busy nearby packing the cones.

'Where are you going now?' one of the pilots asked me.

'Chetwynd. I should be there in four days,' I replied.

'We'll be there in half an hour. Would you like a lift?'

At first I demurred. I didn't need a lift and I would have to return here. Come on, I was urged, just think, you've walked over a thousand miles to meet us just as we're leaving for Chetwynd. What timing! I was soon persuaded and a few minutes later found myself high above the forest in a tiny two-seater helicopter. Below, the Sakunka River wound through the dark forest with snow-spattered ridges rising up on either side. We descended once to refuel at a depot left by the roadside, it being impossible to reach the cone collecting site by road due to the collapse of a number of culverts, Kerry Widsten, the pilot, told me. Then we were back up in the air again, swaying in the strong wind as we crossed a series of ridges that slowly declined in height into the flatter foothills area. To the north a great curl of smoke was drifting up from the forest. Kerry told me it was from a fire started accidentally by an oil survey crew. After half an hour the tiny town of Chetwynd came into view and we dropped down to the airfield. Soon afterwards I was soaking in a warm bath in a motel, rather stunned by the abrupt changes of the day as I'd gone from wading through frozen swamps to being helicoptered out to the luxury of town. Not all was perfect though. My room was above the bar where a live rock band was playing. I was awake until 1am.

A day was spent in Chetwynd on the usual chores, something I'd intended to do when I reached here anyway. Unlike Grande Cache and Tumbler Ridge, Chetwynd (originally called Little Prairie) is a town of the fur trade, one of several set up in the Peace River area in the early nineteenth century. Unfortunately the British Columbia provincial government workers were on strike which meant that the Forest Service office, where I'd hoped to obtain some route advice and maybe better maps, was closed. However the tourist information office was open and here I found a map, the Outdoor Recreation Map of British Columbia No.16: Peace River–Liard Region, that was to be one of my main navigational aids for the rest of the walk. On one side it had the area from Monkman Provincial Park to the Graham River just north of Hudson Hope at a scale of 1:250,000 whilst on the other it continued all the way north to the Liard River at a smaller scale of 1:600,000. I was delighted at my find and tried to buy two copies, one to send home for reference, but the lady who ran the office only had two copies left and she wanted one for her own reference collection. I later obtained a second copy at a lodge on the Alaska Highway. Acting on local advice I also purchased a revoltingly bright orange hat so that I would be seen by hunters. I couldn't imagine wearing it.

On hearing I'd come via Hook Lake the lady in the information centre nodded knowingly and told me in a matter-of-fact way about how she'd had to shoot a black bear that kept raiding her camp when she was there on a fishing trip a few years before. Like the forestry workers I'd met I noticed that she referred to the backcountry as 'the bush', a description I was to find standard from here north and which I adopted myself. I tried to send some mail home including a bulky and heavy packet of used maps and documents but was told that the post offices in Britain were on strike and mail for there couldn't be accepted. This was the first I'd heard about the postal strike and the news had me hurrying back to the motel to phone John Traynor. He confirmed my fears, no mail had been received since the packages I'd posted in Jasper. However, he said, the strike was now over so stuff should start to come through soon. I went back to the post office and persuaded them to take my mail. 'There's no hurry,' I said, 'I won't be home for a month. I just don't want to carry the extra weight.'

Before I could continue north I had to return south along the Sakunka Forest Road, however, a journey that involved a taxi which took me as far as was possible along the increasingly potholed and bumpy road and then, when the taxi could go no further, a lift with a British Columbia rail crew in a pick-up truck that came up behind us. The latter were trying to find out if it was possible to drive all the way to the rail tunnel, where a microwave transmitter needed maintenance. The upper part of the road had been built when the railway was constructed but once it was no longer needed the culverts had been deliberately broken to prevent the road being used and to leave the head of the valley relatively wild, I was told. Because of this the train crew had brought a large eight-wheeled ATV in the back of their pick-up. Sure enough we eventually reached a deep ravine across the road which the pick-up couldn't cross. The ATV could though, so we continued in this incredibly noisy and uncomfortable little vehicle. When there were particularly steep-sided stream beds to cross, two of us got out, leaving just the driver inside, so that we could right the vehicle if it toppled over. Luckily this never occurred. Finally we arrived at the old roadhead by the tunnel and the crew went off to inspect their transmitter whilst I stopped to discuss my route with the forestry workers who were still at the cone collection site, one of whom knew the area well and told me that there were quite a few trails north of Hudson Hope at least as far as the Kwadacha Wilderness though I wouldn't find them marked on the maps. This was welcome and reassuring news and I left feeling more confident of finishing the walk than I had when I'd arrived here two days after the arduous bushwhack along Hook Creek.

Hail and sleet accompanied me as I set off down the old road back towards Chetwynd. After a few hours of head-down marching, the rail crew passed me on their way home, and I passed the helicopter fuel dump. Camp that night was made at dusk by the pleasant Sakunka River, which I was to follow all the way back to Chetwynd. It wasn't the most direct route but I'd had enough of bushwhacking. As I progressed down the valley I passed more and more heavily logged areas and a number of logging camps. Huge trucks roared past at frightening speeds bearing their massive loads to the saw mills in Chetwynd. The whine of chainsaws echoed round the hills. This was the most exploited part of the Rockies I had seen since Crowsnest Pass several months ago. The amount of traffic increased as the road surface gradually improved and I was offered rides frequently. One hunter said he was returning to pack up his camp on the Windfall Creek Recreation Site and he would leave his fire lit for me. When I arrived at the site he was splitting logs to leave for the fire and before he left he gave me a steak, some potatoes and a carton of fresh milk. I had been going to walk a little further but with those provisions I just had to stay. The hunter was interested in my journey but found it hard to understand why anyone would want to walk through the mountains.

As was becoming the evening norm, once I'd eaten I sat by the fire working out plans for the rest of the walk. The back of my journal was filling up with route plans and I'd even sketched in a calendar on which I crossed off the days. Although these sessions gave me a few useful ideas I couldn't really do much serious planning until I reached Hudson Hope and picked up my supply box and set of maps. What thinking ahead did achieve, though, was to reinforce my belief that I could complete the walk, a belief that had taken a battering when I was lost south of Tumbler Ridge and then been shaken again by the Hook Creek bushwhack. I knew that if I lost my confidence that I could do this walk then it would be over, so every time I sat down and worked out what day I thought I would arrive at the finish was a boost to my morale.

I knew I could finish by walking up the Alaska Highway for several hundred miles but this would not be a Rockies walk, neither would it be at all enjoyable. I was determined to walk the last section in the wilderness. My desire to do this was hardened by the six-day road walk from the Sakunka River roadhead to Hudson Hope which I described in my journal as a 'foot-hammering slog'. The day I left the Windfall Creek camp, my third, I walked 23 miles, reading all the way except for the few places where there were some nice views of the river. The series of stepped rapids called Sakunka Falls was the only scene that was at all memorable though. Camp was on the riverbank at a point where it was well away from the road. The area was open and well-used, with fire-rings, a rustic picnic table and a huge shelter frame of tied-together poles. Plenty of cut firewood meant I could have a good blaze, which was needed as by 8.30 it was minus 1°C. The site had a wild feel despite its proximity to the road. In my journal I wrote: 'A huge full moon has risen, a wolf pack howls in the woods across the river and an owl calls this side. Slowly the stars appear . . . a good place to be. A halo round the moon warns of a change in the weather.' Somehow the wolves, the first I had heard, made me feel at home, made me feel that despite the logging this was still, at heart, the Rocky Mountain wilderness.

The second I stuck my head out of the sleeping bag I knew it was cold, the chill air burning my face instantly: minus 7°C read the thermometer. I snuggled back into the warm depths of the sleeping bag, then reached out an arm and pulled in my thermal underwear so it could warm up before I put it on, for even at this temperature I was comfortable sleeping naked, so efficient was my sleeping bag. Once dressed I ventured out into a white frosted meadow where it was minus 11°. I warmed myself up by running round collecting sticks for the very necessary fire. By 9.30, when I set off, a hazy sun had appeared and it was minus 3°. A brisk walk took me the last nineteen miles to Chetwynd, the last few on a paved highway. The day stayed dull and grey and cold with a bitter wind. I wore my hat, fleece sweater and pants and gloves all day. Reaching Chetwynd was a relief. 'Frankly, a tedious day,' reads my journal entry.

The next morning I was interviewed for the local weekly paper *The Pioneer* by reporter Maureen Hawkins. The taxi driver who'd taken me out to the Sakunka Road four days before was the connection and the interview took place in the Les Cabs' office. When I arrived home I found a copy of the paper for October 4th with Maureen's fairly comprehensive interview in it. I seemed to have said several times that I was doing the walk because I enjoyed it. I wonder whom I was trying to convince. Certainly the section from the Sakunka River to Hudson Hope was the least enjoyable part of the walk because it was the only long section (near enough a hundred miles) walked on roads apart from the final stretch. The interview was sandwiched between two breakfasts after which I left Chetwynd for a six-hour, eighteen-mile highway walk to Harv's Resort on Moberly Lake. This wasn't quite half way to Hudson Hope but being on the highway I couldn't just camp where I liked. Luckily I'd found a store with a second-hand book section in Chetwynd as I'd finished the books I had with me during the road walking. Salman Rushdie's *Grimus* and Peter Wright's *Spycatcher* were duly swapped for an Agatha Christie and, a wonderful find this, Thor Heyerdahl's *The Ra Expeditions*. Without anything to read I'd have found the road walking unbearable.

Harv's Resort offered a café and some cabins. The people in the café warned me about the grizzlies north of Hudson Hope. It had apparently been a poor berry season and the bears were hungry. They were shocked when I said I wasn't carrying a gun. So horrified in fact that one of them offered to lend me one saying he'd trust me to return it as he wouldn't rest easily unless he knew I was carrying one. I tried to refuse politely but he was very insistent, producing the weapon in question and showing me how it worked and how light it was. You could use the stock as a walking stick, he said. We finally agreed that I would decide in the morning before I left whether I'd take it or not. I never really had any intention of carrying the gun and slipped off the next morning without mentioning it.

Later in the evening Harv himself turned up and offered some advice on my walk. He didn't think I'd make it as it was too late in the year and deep snow north of the Peace River would stop me. There'd already been several inches at Pink Mountain on the Alaska Highway, he said, and many hunters were coming out of the mountains saying the snow was already too deep. The others present were divided as to whether I'd be eaten by bears or shot by hunters. A final option, thrown in by Harv, was that I'd never get across the rivers. Of these apparent problems the one that really worried me was the last. I'd known all along that there were large unbridged rivers north of the Peace. If I couldn't find a way across any one of them the walk might be over. Still, only by going on would I find out.

A long forgettable day passed on the highway and then I was in Hudson Hope, a month later than I'd planned. In fact on my original schedule I should have finished the whole walk two days earlier. I wasn't bothered, having abandoned that itinerary at Grande Cache. In fact since leaving Jasper my route had not borne much resemblance to the one I'd so carefully worked out back home in England

I was pleased, though, to be north of the Peace River. This, the second largest river in the Canadian Rockies (the largest is the Liard), was of great significance in my mental picture of the walk as it marked the start of the final section. It is geographically significant too, its wide, low-elevation valley separating the northern Rockies from the rest of the range. The river cuts right across the range running eastwards from the huge reservoir of Williston Lake that now fills up much of the Rocky Mountain Trench to the west. I'd left the Continental Divide behind too; south of the Peace it cuts away to the west. All the rivers I would meet to the north end up, like the Peace, in the Arctic Ocean. Hudson Hope (or Hudson's Hope, the two seem interchangeable) lies on the north bank of the Peace. The oldest community in the Rockies, it was founded by Simon Fraser, a partner in the North West Company, in 1805, as a fur-trading post.

In the overview I built up of the walk, Hudson Hope and the Peace River are also important. I saw the walk in terms of two distinct sections: the 'civilised' wilderness of the parks belt south of Grande Cache, and the 'frontier' wilderness north of Hudson Hope. In between lay a transitional area, less well known and controlled than the lands to the south but more visited and less remote than those to the north. Being in Hudson Hope meant I was now facing the greatest challenge of the walk. I had to do some careful thinking and planning before I could continue.

The evening of my arrival I rang Ben and Cia Gadd. I'd checked into the Sportsman's Inn, a Hudson Hope motel, and the owners kindly allowed me to use one of their offices for the phone calls I needed to make as there was no phone in my room. 'We were wondering where you'd got to,' said Ben, as I hadn't contacted him and Cia since Grande Cache. 'I'd like to come up to the Alaska Highway and walk the last few days with you,' said Ben, an offer which I welcomed. He also reassured me about the likelihood of snow during the next month. Not for several weeks yet would it start to pile up, he said.

Stupidly I didn't take my pack when I went along to the post office to collect my two supply boxes, and I had a struggle returning to the motel with them as they weighed sixty pounds between them. Clearly I wasn't going to carry all that! The maps from the Grande Cache box I sent home. The film and the paperbacks I would take with me. Having too many of either was unlikely. There just remained the food. I had twenty-eight days' worth. I couldn't carry more than sixteen days' supplies I decided, so I packed away that amount then sent the remainder off to Ben and Cia who I was sure could find some use for it. I then wrote and sent several letters and postcards as I would now be out of touch for two weeks at least. I had several most welcome letters from family and friends to read and answer too, this being the first contact place since Grande Cache where I'd been over a month ago. The postmistress was most put out when I told her the tourist board had said there was no post office in Hudson Hope, as it had been there since the early years of the century, far longer than the one in Fort St John I'd been told was the nearest.

Knowing I needed local information to plan a feasible route through to the Alaska Highway I rang the nearest Parks and Recreation office which was in Fort St John. They'd get back to me, they said, and soon afterwards I was rung by a Bill Woodhouse who gave me much useful information, the best of which was to contact a Forest Service employee called John Bedell. John, I was told, knew the area really well and should be able to help. I rang him and was immediately inundated with a torrent of information which I hastily scribbled down in my journal. There was an outfitters' trail network north of the Peace, he said, though it wasn't marked on the maps. He outlined a suggested route for me as far as the Kwadacha Wilderness beyond which he had no information. But, he said, I'd find outfitters' camps and a few ranches in the bush. He was sure they'd help me with local information. They might even sell me some food. John felt that I should be able to make it to the Alaska Highway, though not in sixteen days. Three weeks, he reckoned. River crossings could be a problem but they should be low at this time of year, and I might run into snow as I neared the highway. He asked about my trip up to this point. On hearing of my adventure north of the Kakwa River, he laughed. I should have called here not Dawson Creek, he said, he could have told me where the trails were in that area. He went on to say that it was a tough area though, very wet and with dense undergrowth. Although I'd have several cross-country sections in the days to come they'd be much easier than those south of the Peace. The long call ended with my feeling relieved and grateful to have talked to someone who knew the area well and could give me hard information. I felt more certain I could complete the walk than I had for months. I even had a route. The wilderness north of the Peace was no longer a blank.

Above: Looking down Upper Waterton Lake into the USA from the Bear's Hump at the beginning of the walk. Below left: A bear pole with pulleys at Howard Douglas Lake campground, Banff National Park. Middle: A trail sign in Mount Assiniboine Provincial Park. Right: Tree carving of an Indian in the Palliser River Valley.

Above: Mount Assiniboine in the Provincial Park of the same name.
Below: Ball Pass Junction campground, Banff National Park.

Above: On the Rockwall Trail, Kootenay National Park.
Below: The view west from Kiwetinok Pass, Yoho National Park.

Above: The remains of the bridge over Collie Creek.
Below left: Grizzly bear diggings in meadows below Cataract Pass, White Goat Wilderness Area. Middle: ground squirrel on the pack at Jonas Shoulder, Jasper National Park. Right: Porcupines can be a nuisance in camp where they will eat boots and equipment.

Above: Portal Creek campground, Jasper National Park.

Below: The Berg Glacier, Mount Robson Provincial Park.

A beaver dam in Willmore Wilderness Park.

The rickety bridge over the Graham River.

Facing page: Christina Falls, Graham River.

Guides and horses at Big Meadow Camp, Graham River.

Above: Storm and sun in the Northern Rockies.
Below: Looking across Keily Creek to the Great Snow Mountain range.

Through The Northern Wilderness

Hudson Hope to the Alaska Highway
29th September to 19th October   315 miles

On leaving Hudson Hope I had around sixty-five miles of road walking to do before I reached the main ranges of the Rockies which lay well to the west. My aim was to head for and then follow the Graham River, a long waterway that curved west then north back into the wilderness. The first day was spent walking twenty-three miles on gravel and dirt roads past small farms and golden-leaved aspen woods. My pack was the heaviest it had been; indeed for the first time it was completely full. Apart from a good sixteen days' worth of food I was carrying a small library of eight paperback books, many of which, after I'd read them, would be used for lighting fires and as toilet paper in the days to come. I consoled myself with the thought that the pack would never be this heavy again.

There was no water on the route and foolishly I'd set out with none, so by the end of the hot, dusty day I was very thirsty. My destination for the night was Farrell Creek where there was an empty house which the owner of the Sportman's Inn had said I could use. His other business was as a real estate agent and he looked after the place for its absentee owner. At dusk, deer and porcupines appeared on the road, dark shapes against the pale sky. I peered at each one closely in case it was a bear.

It was just about dark when a pick-up heading out of the mountains stopped. The two hunters inside had passed me earlier in the day and wondered what I was doing; on seeing me again they'd decided to ask. When I told them where I was headed, Wayne and Dennis said it was still a long way to Farrell Creek. Why didn't I go back with them to Hudson Hope where they'd put me up for the night and drive me back out here the next day? I could hardly turn down such an offer, so that night I was back in town eating caribou steak and sleeping on Wayne's sofa.

The two hunters were construction workers currently 'between jobs'. Dennis was living out of the back of his pick-up but was planning on

113

building a cabin out in the woods near Mackenzie on the other side of the mountains and spending the winter with a friend on a trap line. The trapping season only ran for two and a half months, he said, but it was possible to earn $100 a day and he enjoyed being in the wilderness. Martens were his main prey, as their pelts were worth most. Both he and Wayne hunted regularly, as I could see from the grizzly hides and mounted elk heads that decorated the walls of the house. They seemed to regard animals as existing only for them to shoot. My own views are both anti-hunting and even more anti-trapping, but I didn't feel I could argue these with people who were doing me a favour and offering friendship and hospitality. I'd first had to face this dilemma on meeting Bruce and Rick at Redwillow Creek but they did not have the clear self-image of themselves as hunters and outdoorsmen that Wayne and Dennis did. I'd discussed this conflict with Ben Gadd when I'd phoned him a few days earlier as I'd realised that just about everyone I met north of the Peace was likely to be a hunter. Ben shared my attitudes to hunting but pointed out that I was now in an area where the old frontier mentality prevailed and I should just accept it and enjoy meeting the characters it threw up.

Whilst I kept quiet about my views on hunting, my hosts were quite voluble when they discovered I wasn't carrying a gun, clearly seeing this as a mark of either unbelievable innocence or else total lunacy. Wayne announced that the danger from bears was so great that he didn't even walk his dog in the fields round his house without taking a rifle along. 'Bears hunt people, you know,' he told me, 'I once shot two grizzlies that were following my scent.' He was so concerned that he gave me a slingshot with which he said I could kill sage grouse if I ran out of food and which just might put off a grizzly. I doubted the latter. It sounded like trying to stop a tank with a bow and arrow but I accepted the slingshot, which reminded me of the catapults I used to make as a boy, and carried it for the rest of the walk. Needless to say it was never used. Wayne was pleased though, feeling that I had at least some protection from the dangers of the bush. I noticed that both of them regarded the wilderness as an essentially hostile, unfriendly place full of danger, where the threat of surprise attack needed to be tamed and conquered—the totally opposite attitude to mine. On foot and carrying no weapons I felt at home in the bush. Even when I'd been lost I hadn't regarded the wilderness as threatening. Any danger came from within myself and it was panic, carelessness or recklessness that I had to guard against. The forests, rivers and mountains were simply there, a neutral world to be experienced and explored, not a hostile monster to be overcome.

More useful than the slingshot was the route advice that I was given, Wayne sketching in tracks on my map that gave a more direct route to the

Graham River, saving at least a day's walk, and avoiding some of the busier logging truck routes. Dennis drove me back out to where they'd picked me up for the start of the hundredth day of the walk. It took me an hour and a half to reach Farrell Creek so I was glad I'd accepted the lift the previous night. I was annoyed though to realise after Dennis had driven off that I'd left my Leki walking stick on Wayne's porch. I missed it instantly, so much so that when I came upon an abandoned roadside hunters' camp soon after setting off I selected an aspen pole as a replacement.

Another day of dirt roads ended in the dark at Kobes Creek where Wayne said there was a trappers' cabin I would be able to use. Just before reaching the creek I'd seen two dark shapes on the road about a hundred yards ahead: a black bear and her cub. Much blowing of my whistle persuaded them to go back into the woods. These were the first bears I'd seen for six weeks, since the one at Blue Creek campground in Jasper National Park in fact. A sunset view of mountains to the west gave me hope of better terrain to come beyond these interminable dirt roads. There were recently abandoned hunters' camps on both sides of Kobes Creek. Wayne had told me that today the moose season in this area closed for the rut until October 16th and so I wouldn't meet many hunters. However moose remains littered the larger of the camps, a sure way of attracting bears, so I used the smaller one. Plenty of cut wood meant I could have a large blaze. Light big fires, they keep the bears away, Wayne had said. The day had been clear and sunny, tee-shirt and shorts weather again. The night was clear and starry. As I sat staring out into the shadows beyond the flickering flames I realised that this was my first night in the wilderness for a week.

The following day was one of the strangest of the walk. It started with my finding a sign in the camp I hadn't used reading 'Beware: Grizzly Crossing Point' and finished with a Christian blessing. The bit in the middle was mundane enough: nine miles of dirt road, cut line and horse trail leading to the Graham River. The only point of interest was when a largish black animal with some smudged white markings descended a steep bank a few yards away and vanished into the undergrowth. It could only have been a wolverine, largest of the weasel family and a secretive creature that I was lucky to see. The wolverine has a reputation as a powerful and fierce creature that will even defend its young against grizzlies. The original fibre-glass version of the Balfour Hut where I'd stayed on the 1987 Wapta Icefields ski tour had been repeatedly wrecked by a wolverine until it was replaced by the current wooden version which the animal couldn't chew its way into. If a wolverine does manage to get into an uninhabited dwelling it will rip up and spray with a foul scent everything it doesn't eat. It is trapped by man for its long guard hairs which don't frost up in cold weather and are therefore ideal for trimming parka hoods.

I came out of the bush on the edge of some large cultivated fields across which I could see a cluster of buildings, beyond which I knew lay the Graham River. I headed for the buildings, and as I approached, a group of people watched me—a situation I was becoming used to. I gave the usual explanation and asked if this was the Federal Ranch, the place I was heading for, but which I shouldn't have reached yet as according to the map it was several miles upstream from where I thought I was (on my map there were no buildings marked at this point). It wasn't the Federal Ranch. This was the Graham River Farm, I was informed. I checked the map; the farm was not marked for some reason but at least my navigation was correct.

The Graham River Farm turned out to be a Christian retreat for training missionaries to work with ethnic minorities and third world peoples as well as a working farm. A scattering of cabins housed the community, one of whom, Heather, told me all about the place and what they were trying to do. At the end of a long conversation in which she tried to convince me that my sojourn in the wilderness was a way of seeking God she suddenly asked if she could bless me. Now I am not a Christian; if I have any beliefs at all they consist, unsurprisingly, of a very vague form of nature worship. Basically though I'm an agnostic inclining towards atheism. However Heather was so sincere that I accepted the blessing as a personal wish for the success of my walk. The conversation with her helped me clarify what the walk was about. I was not, I realised, seeking a truth or revelation about life or God or anything else. In the wilderness I felt content, totally involved in the immediacy of living. There was no hidden mystery, no religious secret waiting to be discovered. The wilderness was itself and that was enough.

Heather and I talked for so long that I ended up staying, sharing a cabin with Bera from Fuji who hoped to bring Christianity to the local Indians. He felt that being a black man he would find it easier to relate to them than a white person would. Whilst I am quite prepared to respect people's religious beliefs I'm highly dubious about the idea of trying to convert others. The strength of these Christians' views frightened me. Can anyone be that right? Their attitudes were a total contrast to those of Wayne and Dennis and I had to admit to myself that I'd felt more at home with the hunters. Again, though, I kept my thoughts to myself, feeling that as a surprise guest who'd been welcomed in I had no right to cause any dissension.

Harold Witmeir, the owner of the farm, showed me round, displaying

116

with pride the machinery and techniques that made the place virtually self-sufficient. He also suggested a different route for the next day that took me north of the Graham for a while to avoid a deep canyon where on his last trip up river, with a horse party twelve years before, the trail had been overgrown and hard to find. He was not aware of anyone going that way since then. The bridge over the Graham having collapsed, visitors and guests of the farm were transported over the river in a tractor-pulled farm cart. I declined this lift however and scrambled over the dilapidated and icy bridge that still remained over the first half of the river, which here divided into two round a large island, before fording the second channel. I then had another road slog of fourteen miles to Blue Grave Creek where I camped on a large hunters' site surrounded by bits of dead moose and mounds of garbage. Nothing of note happened all day apart from a couple of moose, that had somehow avoided the hunters' bullets, running across the road in front of me. I was now in the heart of a heavily logged area and logging trucks and other vehicles had passed constantly all day. One logger in a pick-up stopped to ask what I was doing and expressed total amazement when I told him, removing his baseball cap and scratching his head in disbelief. 'I just don't believe it,' he kept repeating. He'd told me about the site by Blue Grave Creek and that evening he returned to make sure I was all right. This was a purely functional camp but I lit a big fire feeling happy in the knowledge that I was only a few miles from the wilderness proper. My pack wasn't getting much lighter though. I'd been out for four days yet had only eaten one dinner and one breakfast!

My sleep was broken by logging trucks which began roaring by at 3.30am and I was up in the dark at 6.30 to a heavy frost, though the temperature was only minus 1°C. After a last mile on the road I reached a wide cut line with an ATV track down the middle of it, the gateway to the mountains. In my journal that evening I wrote: 'Best day since I left the Willmore Wilderness on September 4th, a month ago . . . hills, unspoilt hills, appeared all around'. I was back in the mountains. I descended back to the Graham River on a wide trail and arrived at the remote homestead of Crying Girl Prairie. I was skirting the fences of this ranch when a grey-haired lady appeared and asked me what I was doing.

'I can't invite you in as the men of the house are away hunting,' she said, 'but I can give you some food.' I was duly loaded up with a bag of home-made cookies, an apple, an orange and a can of Pepsi-Cola. Ever since I'd appeared out of the bush hungry and exhausted at Redwillow campground, everyone I'd met had given me food. It seemed as though it was my reward for surviving the long section on short rations. Before I left I asked whether she'd heard a recent weather forecast. She had, and told me the sunny weather was due to last for at least another three or four days, which was good news.

The wide trail continued beside the river. As I neared a bend a large bull moose walked out into the open in front of me and hacked and tore at the ground with his antlers before running off into the forest with that high-stepping, ungainly trot characteristic of these strange-looking beasts. He was clearly feeling the effects of the rut and I was glad he'd run off as bull moose have been known to attack people at this time of year, regarding them as rivals for the cows, and I'd been warned not to approach too closely to one. The river here was slow and placid, twisting about through a series of reed-filled marshes and little islets. Two moose cows stared at me from the edge of one of the swamps, apparently unconcerned at my presence, enabling me to set up my tripod and take some photographs through the telephoto lens. I made camp on the river's edge on a recently-used site with bough beds and a neatly stacked pile of cut poles but thankfully no garbage. The site was peaceful; for the first time in two weeks there was no sound of traffic.

A pale, delicate dawn slowly lit the river as I set off for the five miles to Christina Falls, a tremendous two-step waterfall in a deep canyon reached by a short, steep-sided trail. Looking at it I reflected that if it was in one of the national parks it would be a major backcountry destination. A couple of miles further and I reached the first outfitters' base camp, that of Christina Falls Outfitters. A wooden gateway led into a large field, on the far side of which stood a ranchhouse sporting, most incongruously, a massive satellite receiving dish. As I walked over the field two men stopped and watched me, one of them through a pair of binoculars. 'Just checking you weren't a grizzly,' he said when I reached them, 'I couldn't believe I was seeing a hiker.' For my part I couldn't believe the attractive ranch buildings I could see all around. Although I knew there were outfitters' camps in the area I was expecting to find tent camps or, at most, small cabins. Only now was I beginning to appreciate the scale of the outfitting business operating in the northern Rockies. The two men were clients, here on a hunting trip, and they introduced me to the proprietor, Darwin Watson, who was in the house.

Once I'd explained (over lunch) why I was walking across his land, Darwin was extremely helpful, marking the trails he knew on my map plus a possible route all the way through to the Alaska Highway. Listening to my stories of the walk he said that he knew the terrain between the Kakwa and Graham Rivers and that it was very rugged with few trails because the scarcity of game meant there were no outfitters operating there. The lack of game he put down to over-hunting due to the number of roads in the area and the use of ATVs. The latter he wouldn't allow to cross his ranch. 'If they ask I tell them they can cross on foot or horseback and hunt higher up the valley but the machines must stay behind.' 'Do they ever do that?' I asked. 'No,' was the reply. Between here and the Alaska Highway the terrain was much easier to cross than that south of the Graham, I was told. The only problem Darwin thought I might have was in fording the Muskwa River which he said was wide, deep and fast. Like John Bedell, whom he knew, he advised against crossing to the west slope into the Kwadacha Wilderness, saying that that region was trailless, rugged and usually very wet.

Darwin also marked the locations of other outfitters' camps on my map plus the names of the main ones. All the camps were manned, he said, as this was the height of the hunting season. 'Call in and I'm sure they'll help you once they've recovered from the shock of seeing a walker out here.' He explained the outfitting system to me saying there were a number of major outfitters each with their own territories rented from the Forest Service which owned the land. Each outfitter ran a base like this one plus a number of wilderness tent or cabin camps. Clients were flown in in light aircraft and then taken out on horses to a smaller camp, which one depending on what they had permits to hunt, those permits being issued to individuals though there were seasons and quotas for different animals. Each hunter went out with a guide whose job it was to lead him to the game. Most camps also employed wranglers to look after the horses. Listening to Darwin I realised that outfitting was big business up here. Most of the outfitters, like Darwin, were descendants of the original pioneers who'd built ranches like this one early in the century and set up the outfitting concerns.

There were two Christina Falls Outfitters' camps further up the Graham valley, Darwin told me, which he had to go off and visit. I was welcome to stay in either of them and he'd tell them I was on my way. With that he left to fly his plane up the valley leaving me to talk to two Swedes, Anna and Haakon, who were working for him. Haakon was a wilderness enthusiast with plans to canoe the Yukon River, who'd found this place by writing to addresses in American hunting magazines he'd bought in Sweden. It was 3.45pm when I left with fifteen miles still to walk if I was to reach the first of Darwin's camps that evening. As I knew the camp was there and the trail was wide and clear, I continued for an hour and a half after dark arriving at Big Meadow Camp at 8.30. This cluster of small log cabins and corrals was much more what I expected an outfitters' camp to look like. I arrived to find I was expected and a hot dinner already on the table. The eight people there were all guides and cooks, as a party was overnighting here on their way back to base having closed down a high-level camp. The last hunters had left with Darwin that afternoon though more were due in the next day. The guides all gave me more route advice, agreeing with

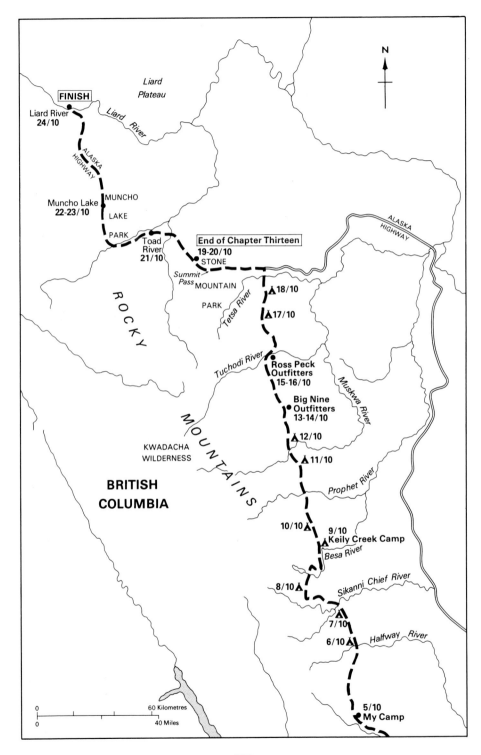

Liard
Plateau

FINISH

Liard River
24/10

Liard River

ALASKA HIGHWAY

MUNCHO

Muncho Lake
22-23/10

LAKE

PARK

Toad
River
21/10

Summit
Pass

R O C K Y

Tetsa River

MOUNTAIN

PARK

End of Chapter Thirteen
19-20/10
STONE

△18/10

△17/10

ALASKA HIGHWAY

N

Tuchodi River

●**Ross Peck
Outfitters**
15-16/10

Muskwa River

M O U N T A I N S

●**Big Nine
Outfitters**
13-14/10

△12/10

KWADACHA
WILDERNESS

△11/10

**BRITISH
COLUMBIA**

Prophet River

10/10△

9/10
△**Keily Creek Camp**

Besa River

8/10△

Sikanni Chief River

△
7/10

6/10△   Halfway   River

0   60 Kilometres

0   40 Miles

5/10
My Camp

Darwin that river fords would by my biggest problem though they were also concerned about bears, whereas Darwin had said I'd be lucky to see one and highly unlikely to have any problems with any. That night I slept on a bunk bed in one of the cabins. This walk through the remote wilderness of the northern Rockies was becoming quite a luxury trek!

As a pink dawn broke over the still-distant mountains I watched the guides packing up their horses for departure, strapping on saddles, rifles, bedrolls and large red-painted wooden boxes marked in white paint with the words 'Christina Falls Outfitting'. Loaded up with more food I set off on a newly-cut trail beside the river, again wearing shorts and a tee-shirt. In a clearing two caribou watched me curiously from close quarters, the first I'd seen since the ones in Jasper National Park. They were much further south than suggested in *The Handbook,* which gave their range as only being from the Kwadacha Wilderness north. I was to grow used to seeing these creatures of the great north woods and the arctic tundra at close quarters over the next few weeks but the thrill of being able to observe them in their natural surroundings never faded. Soon after seeing the first two I came across a grizzled old buck with one huge antler, the other being no more than a short stub, who allowed me to take several photographs before wandering off. Whilst taking these pictures I realised that my flat-topped aspen staff made a crude but usable monopod for steadying my camera when I had the telephoto lens attached. This discovery was to enable me to take a number of wildlife pictures I would not otherwise have obtained in the days to come. I only wished the rather obvious idea of using my walking stick as a monopod had occurred to me earlier in the walk. The reason it hadn't was probably that the Leki stick I'd used most of the time was shorter and had a rounded handle. By a stroke of luck the aspen staff was just the right height to be used without my having to bend or crouch, both awkward with the pack on.

Regular river fords would, I knew, be the norm through this region so I was not surprised at the ten crossings I had to make between Big Meadow and the next camp, known confusingly as My Camp. The problem with all these crossings, though, was that changing into trainers for each one took up too much time. This day I wore my trainers all the time. In the future, though, I just gave up trying to keep my boots dry and did the fords in them, using the trainers as dry footwear in camp. I missed the last ford before My Camp and was bushwhacking up the wrong bank when I was hailed by two horsemen on the far side of the river. They were very amused when I simply waded straight across to them. Follow us to the camp, they said. I did so and we soon arrived at a tent camp set up on a large cleared area where there had been a forest fire. My Camp consisted of three large white canvas ridge tents and one four-pole lean-to which I slept in with one of the hunters. The pair I'd met had been Stubby, a local Indian who was the head guide, and his current client who, having shot a moose that day, was feeling quite pleased.

In one of the tents I met Marge, a middle-aged lady who was the camp cook. She lived here, sleeping on a raised wooden platform in one corner and surrounded by food. She kept a rifle by her bed, just in case, she said, a bear came round during the day when she was alone in camp or in the middle of the night when everyone was asleep. An extension housed a preparation table whilst a large picnic table in the main tent was set for dinner. A black tin wood stove, its chimney pipe poking out through a hole cut in the roof, stood in one corner with pans and cutlery hung all around it. The aroma of freshly made coffee wafted round the tent from a pot on the stove .and Marge immediately offered me a cup. I was astonished at the quality of the food Marge could make on the seemingly uncontrollable stove; she produced everything from three course dinners to cakes and cookies. The food I ate in the outfitters' camps was in fact better than any I had had in a restaurant and a far cry from the bacon and eggs and greasy fry-ups I had imagined would be standard fare. That evening at dinner there were four hunters and three guides, one of the hunters going out that night with Darwin who flew in just before dark. I went outside to watch him leave. The tiny plane trundled down the rough runway that had been hacked out of the forest and laboured into the air, just clearing the tree tops. I was quite glad I was walking. A fire having been lit I hung out my wet socks and trainers in the hope they'd dry, then stood round under the starry sky talking to the hunters and guides. One of the latter, Butch, wore a large cowboy hat with a feather in it and told many tall stories of his adventures in the mountains. I could imagine that having him as a guide would make for an entertaining time.

Pancakes, maple syrup, bacon and coffee made for a superb breakfast on a beautiful minus 2 degree morning. Marge was very worried I'd starve and wouldn't let me leave without loading me up with two packed lunches consisting of three wholemeal bread cheese sandwiches, a pancake filled with jam, a bag of cookies, several thick slices of delicious chocolate cake and an orange. She told me she was from southern Alberta where her friends had been horrified when she told them she was coming to work this far north and in the wilderness too. 'They think it's all eskimos up here!' she said. When I left she accompanied me to the first creek crossing asking on the way if I was taking vitamin pills. It turned out she was interested in holistic medicine and reflexology. My simplistic and uninformed notions of what to expect in outfitters' camps were certainly being shaken up.

I finally left the Graham River behind at a boggy timberline col and descended on an excellent trail to the Halfway River. I was now in the heart of the mountains again with peaks all around including the shapely 7700-foot-high Mount Laurier to the east and 8369-foot glacier-flanked Mount Robb and the main crest of the Rockies to the west. The peaks here are not as high as those south of the Peace River, the highest being around the 9800-foot mark (Ben Gadd reckons that Mount Smythe in the Kwadacha Wilderness is probably the highest peak in the area though no-one knows for sure as most summit elevations haven't been verified. Another candidate is Mount Ulysses in the Great Snow Mountain group which I was to see in a few days' time). As timberline runs from 5500 feet at the Peace River to 4900 feet at the Alaska Highway, compared with around 7250 feet in Banff and Jasper Parks, the actual rise from timberline to the summits is the same, making the mountains look just as impressive.

The Halfway River was easily forded being no more than a small creek, and once across I camped by a good trail in the forest on a flat piece of ground. Others had used it in the distant past, as was shown by a number of half-buried rust-rotten cans I found. Hanging my food was a problem as the lodgepole pines I was camped under were small and their branches wouldn't bear the weight of my hardly diminished supplies. It took an hour before I managed to haul the food up over a branch that didn't break.

A red dawn heralded an overcast sky that soon brought bits of drizzle. I'd been told that a good horse trail ran north from the Halfway about here but that the point of departure from the valley wasn't clear, so I spent half an hour quartering the hillside until I found it. The time was worthwhile for the trail was excellent and took me easily if steeply up to a superb alpine landscape. 'Lots of peaks and lots of pics,' I wrote in my journal. I crossed a large open bowl before beginning the descent as the sky began to clear. The ground was open and there was a plethora of horse and game trails to follow. Two small pretty waterfalls tumbling into clear pools revealed themselves as I descended through woods and meadows to a bigger creek. I realised that one of the joys of walking through this region was that I didn't know what to expect. There were no signposts, no guidebooks, no viewpoints. I literally had no idea what might lie round the next corner, over the next hill and in the next valley. After a shallow ford of Sidonius Creek I climbed back uphill to a burnt area that I remembered Darwin mentioning. I camped on the edge of this with a good view of the mountains to the south and at the head of Sidonius Creek. A tiny creeklet provided water. Although a gusty wind was shaking those dead trees that were still standing it wasn't cold, still +2°C at 8pm.

Sitting by a fire which I kept small due to the sparks that the wind whipped everywhere, I worked out that I was about half way between Hudson Hope and the Alaska Highway. I'd been walking for nine days though the first four of those had been on roads and good tracks. The hardest terrain was still to come. The extra food I was being provided with by the outfitters looked like proving essential if I was to finish this section without going hungry. I hoped my gear would last too. My trail pants were in shreds from bushwhacking and my crude stitching was only just holding them together whilst most of my socks had holes in them. Most worrying though was the pack as the plastic section connecting the hipbelt to the frame had begun to crack. Despite these concerns I felt content as I sat and stared at the starry sky and the line of jagged peaks on the horizon.

During the night the wind strengthened and I was up at half past midnight pegging out the tent guylines and checking that nothing had blown away. The wind dispersed the clouds, though, to give a pleasantly softly lit dawn. I continued on up through the gaunt dead forest of smooth grey-white, bark-free tree trunks and blackened limbs until eventually I re-entered live green trees shortly before arriving at Embree Creek. Although I was travelling cross-country the going was fairly easy with little deadfall and not much undergrowth in the open forest. It continued this way as I followed the creek to a small lake on a high saddle and then descended via Bartle Creek to the Sikanni Chief River. Across this lay the massive castellated cliffs of Mount Bertha whilst upstream I could see a fine snow-splashed pyramid-shaped peak resembling Mount Assiniboine that wasn't marked on my map. I crossed the Sikanni Chief via a barely knee-deep paddle to find a good trail in a cut line heading north. This took me to Colledge Creek above which I camped on a small shelf with glorious mountain views to the west. During the day I'd seen fifteen caribou in groups of five, four, three, two and one!

The track became a narrower trail as I passed Cranswick Lake and descended to the Besa River. The ford of this wide river by the remnants of an old bridge was cold and knee-deep but easy. Once across I found a well-used ATV track which I expected, as upstream lay Redfern Lake which I'd been told was a popular destination for anglers. I took this trail a short way until it recrossed the river and continued south-east to Trimble Lake. Here the Besa is forced north by a mountain barrier through a narrow valley. I was to follow it until it turned east again, mostly on game trails and with four more fords, necessitated by small bluffs and cliffs. As I neared Keily Creek, where I knew there was a Besa River Outfitters' camp, I found a well-used trail which I followed to an airstrip, where a young male moose was grazing, and then into the camp. As I stepped out of the trees I could see a half-circle of people standing round a fire facing me with several cabins behind them. As I walked towards them the sound of their voices died and they all stared at me. I felt very self-conscious but didn't speak until I was close enough not to have to shout. When I said 'Hello', there was a moment of silence as the group of hunters and guides stared at me open-mouthed, unable to believe their eyes. The expected question finally came. 'Where the hell did you come from?' For once it was one of the hunters, a big heavily-built American from New York State called Jim Jackson, who invited me to stay. Again I was given dinner, breakfast and two packed lunches.

Unlike the other camps though, this one had an uneasy air about it. The hunters were not completely happy with the way things were going. They were all well-off white men from the USA whilst the guides were all local Indians and there was clearly little communication between the two groups. The camp was closing down for the season in two days' time, to the relief of the guides who'd been here for two months. 'We're counting the minutes,' said one, 'we haven't seen our children for too long.'

After dinner I stood by the fire listening to the hunters talking. One of them was reminiscing about his days as a sniper in the Vietnam war. The others had ribbed him a little about his failure to bag a moose and he was clearly trying in some way to prove himself to them. Even so, his stories of shooting 'gooks' profoundly disturbed me. How could someone talk so casually about killing other human beings? I even detected a hint that he'd enjoyed doing it. The hunter cuffed the earth with his boot.

'I can shoot the eye out of a frog at a hundred paces,' he announced, continuing rather plaintively, 'so why can't I get my moose?'

'Maybe it's frogs you should be hunting,' said someone else, to general laughter. The hunter looked down and scowled.

Jim invited me to his cabin for a late coffee and told me how he'd just returned from big game hunting in Zimbabwe and a visit to Britain. Once, he said, he'd been deer hunting is Scotland but he didn't like the fact that you couldn't shoot the finest beasts but only the ones the stalkers allowed you to. The next morning I was to see what the finest beasts were when all the antlers from the slaughtered animals were displayed together. The local hunters I'd met round the towns hunted for food for their table. These were trophy hunters, seeking displays for their office walls. Success was measured in the span of the antlers or the number of 'points'. I couldn't understand why anyone would want to kill such magnificent creatures. There wasn't even any skill involved that I could see, given the nature of modern high-velocity rifles. If I'd been so inclined I could have killed many moose, caribou, elk and other animals in the last few weeks. Instead I'd taken photographs. As usual however I kept my thoughts to myself.

I started the night on a bunk in the guides' cabin but it was so hot that by 12.30 I'd moved outside to bivvy under a tree. The guides thought I was crazy but I was much more comfortable. After a huge breakfast the next morning Jim gave me some cuppa-soups, bread sticks and packets of raisins. Still not sure how long it would take me to reach the Alaska Highway I was not turning down any food. The guides showed me where the trail was and warned me I might find the Prophet River, a day or so's walk to the north, hard to cross and that I should watch out for moose kills near the trail as they might have been taken over by grizzlies. They offered me a horse ride over Keily Creek itself so I could start the day with dry feet. Foolishly I accepted, even though it would mean a few yards I wouldn't have walked. My pack went across first, strapped to a saddle. When the guide tried to remove it from the horse the animal spooked and ran round in circles, the pack hanging off it by the hipbelt as I watched in horror. Once across, the horse being happier with me than it had been with the pack, I found as I suspected that the cracked plastic connector had now broken in two. I tried to fix it but hadn't the tools so I forded the river and returned to the camp to borrow a wrench. Still unable to undo the central nut I went back again for some pliers. On this occasion I met Jim who gave me a roll of duct tape. 'This stuff'll hold a car together,' he said. I forded the creek for the fourth time and strapped up the hipbelt with the tape before finally setting off. Of course it's possible that this episode was a blessing in disguise as the hipbelt would probably have ripped out eventually, perhaps high in the mountains where there was nobody with a handy roll of duct tape to come to my aid. All in all, though, I didn't leave Keily Creek Camp with too many fond memories.

A long, hot, sweaty climb taken at a fast pace fuelled by my anger at the incident that had just taken place took me above timberline and to a view that wiped out all my negative thoughts in an instant. Around the head of Keily Creek was ranged a magnificent alpine panorama dominated by the white dome of the Great Snow Mountain and the rock spires of Mounts Circe and Ulysses. I felt so excited and inspired by this view that I left the pack and climbed up a nearby hill for a better view. I then stayed above timberline for most of the rest of the day meandering over low cols, round the heads of wooded valleys and along broad ridges through a complex area that needed a 1:50,000 topographic map to interpret properly. Not having one I just headed north on game trails or cross-country on the easiest line. High cirrus in the morning led to stratus by mid-afternoon along with cool winds, so it was on with shirt and long pants in place of the shorts and tee-shirt I'd started off wearing.

Towards evening I descended into a creek valley that contained the worst terrain I'd encountered north of the Peace River: very boggy, mossy and tussocky with much deadfall. I picked up a succession of game and long disused horse trails but the walking was still hard work and progress slow. Even though it was growing dark I had to continue, as the

126

steep-sided valley had no places for a camp. I reached the wide east–west running Richards Creek valley and flat ground just after 6.30pm and soon found an old horse camp where I gratefully stopped. I knew there was an outfitters' camp up the valley and I could hear horse bells so it couldn't be far, but I wasn't continuing in the dark when there was no need and I was tired. I'd pushed hard all day and my right foot was very painful. I'd also arrived at the site soaked in sweat and began to shiver as soon as I stopped—the temperature being a degree below freezing—so I lit a big fire. The sky was clear now with many stars and I sat round the fire drinking coffee, quite happy not to be in an outfitters' camp. During the day I'd seen twenty-two caribou, one more than the day before.

I was up in the half-light (it wasn't fully light now until 7am) having been woken by squirrels chattering and birds singing. The temperature in the tent was minus 4°C. Some thin high clouds made for a pink subdued dawn. Half an hour after starting out I arrived at the outfitters' camp. I hadn't realised I was that close. It was in a beautiful setting with mountains all around. Like Keily Creek Camp it was closing in two days' time and there were just two guides, two hunters all the way from Texas and a cook here. A week later and I'd have found many of these camps shut down. I was invited in for a second breakfast and lightly berated for not having arrived the night before! The cook told me that this camp was run by Prophet River Outfitters which was owned by a USA consortium. She thought hunting was in decline due to over-shooting and that outfitters would have to offer backpacking and wilderness trips to stay in business. The guides here reckoned that crossing the Muskwa River would be easy as there had been no rain for a while and water levels were low. I hoped they were right.

I departed on a good trail clutching a bag of assorted chocolate bars to cross a wide boggy saddle and descend to the Prophet River, the first of the major fords. The slow, swirling river with its muddy bed was easy to cross due to the weak current although it was thigh-deep and very wide. Having braced myself for a shock of cold water I was amazed to discover the river was pleasantly warm. A quick dive into *The Handbook* on the far bank revealed that there were hot springs along the Prophet though under 'comments' was written tersely 'no information'. They were clearly upstream of where I was anyway.

The day ended in confusion. I went wrong on leaving the Prophet, despite Darwin's clearly remembered advice, and didn't go far enough east along the valley before heading north. This left me following game trails to a small lake on the watershed between the Prophet and Muskwa valleys. When I first saw the lake from a distance it looked a good place to camp but when I arrived on its shores I found the surrounding area boggy and lumpy. A camp here would be most uncomfortable. A couple of moose took off through the trees. This was ideal terrain for them. As I watched them head up the hillside I saw a white patch high above the lake looking remarkably like a cabin. I struggled up the steep slopes in fading daylight to find a locked prefabricated hut with oil drums and other rubbish scattered around. Looking inside I could see from the shelves of samples and pinned-up notices that it was an oil exploration survey building, which explained all the coloured flagging I'd seen in the nearby woods. There was no water nearby and the hut was unusable as a shelter so I dropped back down to the lake again to pick up a good trail at its outlet. I followed it down into the night-shrouded forest, walking by the light of my head torch. Just after the trail crossed the outlet creek I stopped and cast around for a camp site in the dense spruce forest. Eventually I managed to squeeze the tent in between two trees and set up my kitchen a little lower down the slope. This was very much an emergency camp and didn't seem very comfortable but as I wrote in my journal: 'at least I'm in the Muskwa drainage now.' I failed to hang my food for the first and only time on the walk. The reasons, as I wrote in my journal, were: 'branches breaking, rocks falling off, me falling over'. It was after the last episode when I'd gone flying backwards onto hard ground after the line suddenly pulled free from the branch it had been tangled up in that I stopped, concerned I would hurt myself. I left the food sacks wedged high up on a branch. As I was returning to the tent a noise disturbed me, the noise of an animal breathing heavily nearby. Unable to see anything I ran back to the tent and stoked up the remnants of the small fire I'd lit earlier. It could have been a bear though it was more likely to have been a porcupine. It scared me anyway. The day had been cloudy with the mountains dark and hazy but by 10.30pm it was clear with a warm breeze, the temperature being five degrees.

It was only one degree at 8am with a dull, windless dawn. I was a long way down the trail before anywhere that would have made a better camp appeared, so I felt glad I'd stopped when I had. As I descended I put up three moose, one a fine heavily-antlered bull. Then, as I neared the Muskwa River, mountains began to appear including a huge wall of them across the valley in front of me. I headed west on the trail at first by mistake and had to backtrack, but this diversion did give me a good view of the upper Muskwa valley and the distant peaks of the Kwadacha Wilderness to the north-west. I forded the river, the one I was most concerned about, easily at a wide section. It was much colder with a stronger current than the Prophet and had a firm pebble base. To keep them all dry I removed my boots, socks and trousers and crossed in a pair of dirty socks, an idea I'd picked up from the book I was reading, Mike

Tomkies' *A Last Wild Place,* about wildlife in the Scottish highlands. He'd first done this though when crossing creeks in the coastal mountains of northern British Columbia, due west from the Rockies. I noted with interest not to say alarm his comment that the book he'd written on his Canadian adventures had been turned down by his publisher because the latter didn't believe he'd travelled alone through grizzly country. I hoped the book I was intending to write wouldn't meet the same fate. The socks trick worked quite well and I wondered why it hadn't occurred to me before. I was very relieved at the easy ford as I wasn't expecting any more serious river crossings. I felt as though the last barrier that might have prevented me finishing the walk had fallen.

I followed the river north, to camp at the head of the wide valley that runs over to Gathto Creek where I was heading the next day. Although it was fairly early (4.45pm) I was reluctant to leave the river in case there was no water for a while and nowhere to camp. A well-used but clean horse site on the bank looked very appealing after the previous night's makeshift camp. There was plenty of flat ground and a pile of charred logs for a fire. A barred owl called from a nearby tree. Three snow buntings flitted along shingle banks beside the river and on going to fetch water I noted some bear tracks. This night my food was securely hung however. I was to be glad it was at 4.30am when I was woken by the sound of snapping branches nearby. I lay in the sleeping bag wondering if it was a bear. Until I found out I knew I wouldn't sleep any more so after a few minutes I reluctantly got up, making a lot of noise in the process, before, singing loudly, I unzipped the door and peered out of the tent. The beam of my head torch lit up patches of the tree trunk and the dead ashes of the fire but no bears. A little further away I could see the grey, cold waters of the river rushing past. I went outside and checked that the food bags were still there, which they were, and then, the noise a mystery, I returned to bed.

It was barely light at 7am, the dawn cold and grey under total cloud cover. There was much cheerful bird song however, including the chatter of two gray jays that flitted round the site. Then somewhere downriver an elk stag bugled, a weird rutting call that consists of a rising series of grunts and whistles. From the Muskwa I had some very difficult terrain to cross, 'a terrible slog through burn and deadfall to Kluachesi Lake,' I wrote in my journal. At the large lake, yet another on a wide pass on an east-west running ridge, I found a good, well-used and blazed outfitters' trail which I followed steeply north-westwards to a high col, well above timberline, that gave extensive views of dark peaks under threatening clouds. As I reached the col five caribou raised their heads and then started to walk towards me. For once I had to change my telephoto zoom lens hurriedly for a shorter focal length one in order to photograph them. Eventually they

129

ambled off, after staring intently at me, presumably satisfied that whatever I was I wasn't dangerous. A few minutes later I looked down the far side of the col into a tree-dotted alpine bowl to see nine moose heading uphill together, a most unusual sight as moose are solitary animals that normally stay in the valley bottoms.

I lost the trail on the col but picked it up again soon after descending to timberline. I was puzzled however when it turned eastwards and took me almost all the way back to Kluachesi Lake. I stayed on it however as it made for fast, easy travel, reasoning that it must be part of a loop hunters used to reach the high country. Once back near the lake the trail split, one branch heading north, the other south. An elk hind bounded away across a boggy meadow as I took the northbound path. Again I found myself descending a steep-sided, narrow valley with nowhere to camp and again I continued on into the night. At dusk it began to rain and I was quite wet by the time I reached Gathto Creek. I knew that there was an outfitters' camp upstream and I could hear horse bells, which meant it wasn't far away, so I decided to head there rather than make camp in the dark and rain. First I had to cross the creek which I did, quite recklessly as I was too tired to be careful, by simply plunging in and wading through it, the beam of my head torch lighting up speckled rocks and dark swirls of water. The creek was cold but no more than knee-deep and I was soon stumbling along the wide trail on the other side towards the bright lights I could see in the distance. After what seemed hours I came out of the wet, dripping trees to see a cluster of buildings, fences and corrals in front of me with electricity wires strung on poles and in the centre a brightly-lit, quite imposing alpine-style lodge. This was not the small wilderness camp I'd expected.

Now I was here I had no option but to find a way through the maze of fences and gates to the house. As I did so I was aware of a figure standing in the shadows just inside the door watching me. This turned out to be Barry Tompkins, proprietor of Big Nine Outfitters whose base I'd just walked into. In the way I'd become accustomed to, and was almost taking for granted, he welcomed me in after a brief explanation on my part and sat me down in front of a large meal. The surroundings were not what I was used to at all though, the lodge being as imposing inside as it was out, a beautiful building with huge painted wildlife murals on the walls. I slept that night in the large guides' cabin.

Rain continued to fall all night turning to sleet by dawn and heavy snow soon afterwards. The previous evening Barry had invited me to spend a day here but I'd declined. 'I think you'll be staying after all,' he said in the morning. He was right. Going on in this blizzard when I had a safe, comfortable haven to sit it out in would have been very unwise. Also I felt my body could do with the rest. Since leaving Hudson Hope I'd walked non-stop for fifteen days and 250 miles, the longest section of the walk without a break. In my journal I wrote of the day off: 'I needed it as my ankles were sore this morning. I feel I'm running down.'

Big Nine offered a wealth of facilities including a laundry and a shower so I was able to wash myself and my clothes for the first time since Hudson Hope. The main generator being out of order this did mean using a petrol generator and a rather complex system of inlet and outlet pipes especially for the laundry but just to have such devices out here was quite something.

The storm kept nearly everybody in camp and I spent much of the day talking to the hunters who were here and to Barry. Two of the hunters, Theresa and Lewis Mull, were from the USA where Lewis had a chain of outdoor stores. He was also one of the original shareholders in the equipment company The North Face, some of whose gear I had used though I had none with me on this trip, and we had an enjoyable discussion about the outdoor trade which reminded me that in just three weeks' time I was supposed to be covering Britain's annual trade show, the Camping and Outdoor Leisure Association exhibition in Harrogate, for *Odyssey* magazine. I found it hard to imagine spending three days inside over-heated halls looking at outdoor gear instead of being out here using the stuff.

I talked to Barry about the outfitting business and its future, thinking of the comments about hunting being on the decline that I'd heard at the Richards Creek camp. Barry felt that hunting would continue but that there was obviously a limit to the game that could be taken without stocks becoming depleted. This is the big game mecca of North America, he said, and famous amongst hunters worldwide, but there is a limit to how many animals they could shoot without ruining the area. Big Nine, he told me, was named after the nine big game animals that could be hunted in the territory namely: elk, moose, caribou, bighorn sheep, mountain goat, grizzly bear, black bear, wolf and wolverine. The overheads of running an operation like this with only two seasons, a month or so in the spring and three months in the autumn, plus a one-to-one guide to hunter ratio and flying in clients in small groups in light aircraft meant that the costs to the hunters were very high. Most clients were American, Japanese and European businessmen, very few were Canadians. Barry would like more Canadians to come hunting but said the price was just too high. He also wanted to extend his season by offering activities other than hunting and he showed me a new colour brochure listing wilderness skills ('not military-type survival courses,' he stressed) and photography trips. This seemed to me a good idea and I hope he's successful in attracting clients. It would be nice to think that eventually the outfitters could stay in business running ventures that did not involve slaughtering the local wildlife.

Barry also told me of the outfitters' worry about the future of this vast and relatively untouched wilderness. He saw mining exploration for oil or coal or gas as the big threat. Even if no actual extraction went ahead the tracks left behind opened up the area to ATVs and this ease of access would mean over-hunting and over-use. This was why he, like Darwin Watson on the Graham River and, he said, other outfitters would not allow ATVs to cross their land. Most outfitters owned the land immediately round their bases, land originally settled by their parents or grandparents, though most of the area was in the hands of the Forest Service. Logging though is not a threat as the timber is not of a high enough quality to be worth the effort required to take it out of such remote areas.

Because there is no protection for the region other than its inaccessibility—except for small areas like the Kwadacha Wilderness—the outfitters were putting together a plan for a designated wilderness extending from the Graham River to the Alaska Highway with provision for the continuance of their business. They had Forest Service backing for this plan but there was strong opposition from the coal and oil lobby. I was very heartened to hear that an attempt was being made to preserve the area and I hope the proposed wilderness comes about soon, before the nibbling away at the edges that is currently taking place grows in extent and ruins this unique and vast wilderness forever. After my discussion with Barry I feel that he at least is genuinely concerned for the future of an area he loves and wishes to see untouched rather than just being concerned for the future of his business. Having now walked through most of it I was very aware that the Graham River-Alaska Highway region is the largest unspoilt and undeveloped part of the Rockies left and that maintaining it as such is of vital importance. Nowhere else in the whole of the Rockies chain from New Mexico north had I felt such a sense of wilderness, of remoteness, of a natural world far from the concerns and petty squabbles of human society. There are only a few such places left on earth and I feel they must be preserved if we are to have a chance of retaining our connection with and understanding of nature, a relationship that I believe is crucial if the human race is to survive. I also believe that whether humanity has a future or not we have no right to destroy the natural environment and the wildlife that depends upon it.

The storm started to disintegrate at dusk and night came with a hard frost and a black starry sky over the almost luminous whiteness of the pale hills. I hoped I would be able to reach the highway, which still lay over sixty miles away, before the real storms of winter began. This one, I felt, was just a foretaste of what was soon to come.

Barry was most concerned that I should have a successful trip and provided me with lots of food and new batteries for my headlamp which had seen rather more use than I thought it would. Then on the morning I left he gave me a Big Nine tee-shirt and an embossed Big Nine clasp knife as mementos of my visit.

The day was cold though I was warm enough on the steep climb out of the Gathto Creek valley. Even so I wore my shell jacket over my fleece sweater all day and donned my wool mitts, bought so long ago in Grande Cache, for the first time over my thin gloves. The snow, which was now lying well below timberline, was about four inches deep and wet as a slight thaw was starting, so my feet were soon damp and very cold. The leather of my boots had started to split and one of the soles was coming off at the toe so they had no longer any semblance of waterproofness. What I really needed, but didn't have, were gaiters to keep the snow out of my boots and to keep my socks dry.

From a view of cold white mountains I descended cross-country to the cheerfully named Dead Dog Creek where I picked up a good trail that took me over undulating terrain to the Tuchodi River. The day's total of wildlife sightings was four caribou, three moose and three elk, two of the latter being fine stags who were lucky I was only shooting them with a camera. Melting snow meant the Tuchodi was high and strong and it took me some time to find a crossing point, which I finally did where the river was heavily braided. Even so I had to take great care in the thigh-deep swirling currents of the larger channels. I had been a little premature in thinking my river fording problems were over when I crossed the Muskwa. Once over I headed east along the bank into a wall of dense fog and, yet again, into the night. I was aiming for the next outfitter's cabin, that of Ross Peck, not that I needed food or accommodation but because Barry Tompkins had said Ross should be able to suggest a route north from the Tuchodi to the Alaska Highway, an area he didn't know. I arrived just as dinner was finishing so Ross and his clients were seated round the table when I knocked on the door, having located the camp by the lights I could just make out through the darkness and fog. A voice called me in. I opened the door to see two rows of faces staring at me open-mouthed.

Over a hot meal I told my story. I never felt tired of doing so because of the interest that was always shown in my walk by the outfitters and their clients. After I'd finished Ross asked me where I was from.

'Let me guess,' he said, 'Australia? New Zealand?'

'He's from England,' came a voice from a backroom. 'You should be able to tell, you've been married to an Englishwoman for long enough.' With that, Deborah Ross appeared. She was from Cumbria and had met Ross in Vancouver where he'd been studying wild life biology, returning to take over the outfitting business when his father died. By now my original idea that outfitters would be Davy-Crockett-style throwback pioneer types had been proven so wrong that meeting one who was a wildlife biologist and had an English wife didn't surprise me at all. Ross went over my route with me and made some suggestions for reaching the highway which he thought would take three or four days. I would pass one more outfitters' camp he said but it would probably be closed as the season was over. However he was sure it would be all right for me to stay there as long as I left everything as it was.

Ross turned out to be very involved in the wilderness designation plan and said he expected to spend most of the winter working on it. He told me a draft was due to be published soon. He had no plans however to offer any trips other than hunting ones and said he did little advertising, relying instead on clients' returning year after year. He wanted, he told me, to keep the business small and low-key. His father, Bob, had been a noted local outfitting pioneer, indeed a nearby peak had just been renamed Mount Peck in his honour.

A cabin with a wood stove was provided for me so I was able to dry out my wet boots and socks and air my gear. Deborah had regular deliveries of the weekly *Manchester Guardian* digest in order to keep up with the news at home and she lent me a great pile of these to browse through which meant I stayed up quite late, reading and catching up on news of the world outside.

Ross suggested I stay a day as another big storm was forecast and he and Deborah made me feel so at home that I was reluctant to leave. As at Big Nine I felt as though I was physically running down and needed a long rest. But for now another day off was welcome. After breakfast Ross skimmed through *The Handbook,* which he hadn't seen before, pointing out a few inaccuracies regarding wildlife in this area. He told me that in the Sikinni Chief drainage there was a large herd of buffalo, seven hundred or more strong he estimated, the descendants of ones released there by a local outfitter. Their ownership was now a matter of dispute between the provincial government and the outfitter. In the meantime these buffalo, whose existence was unknown to the outside world, continued to prosper. This was news, as according to *The Handbook* there were only two captive herds in paddocks in Banff and Waterton National Parks plus a few smaller herds and individual animals in ranches on the fringes of the mountains left in the Rockies. Only one free-ranging buffalo was known in 1986, wrote Ben, and that was a female escapee from a ranch that had been seen in eastern Jasper National Park.

Throughout my walk in the northern Rockies I heard tales of a 1930s expedition organised by a French-American millionaire that had tried to cross the mountains and reach the Pacific Ocean in half-track vehicles in order to show that building a road through the region was feasible. Ross Peck knew a great deal about this venture and showed me a copy of a hand-written journal by a local man who'd taken part together with a newspaper report of the time. There seemed to be a great deal of mystery surrounding the Bedaux Expedition (named after its leader), with many doubts as to the real reasons behind it. What nefarious purpose could be served by trying to cross miles of wilderness I find it hard to imagine but certainly the end met by Bedaux himself suggests there may have been some hidden motive behind the expedition. Before coming to the Rockies he'd led an expedition across the Sahara Desert and on the outbreak of the Second World War he returned to North Africa where he was arrested as a Nazi spy. Whilst in prison he committed suicide. Whatever the reasons behind it, though, the Bedaux Expedition was a lavish affair that poured large sums of money into local businesses and gave employment to many local people. As it took place at the height of the depression it became a major factor in the economy of the area. Indeed Ross Peck reckons its effects can still be felt, many local concerns having been founded on Bedaux money. The expedition itself was a partial success, a way being found across the Rockies but the trek foundering before it reached the Pacific. The half-tracks often had to be dragged through boggy ground and horses were used much of the time. Today when outfitters want to bring heavy machinery into their camps they do it in winter when the ground is frozen. Barry Tompkins had told me how it had taken four days to drive a bulldozer from the highway to the Big Nine camp one winter. On looking through the accounts of the expedition I found I'd followed its route in places, It's remembered in the names of the region by Bedaux Pass in the Kwadacha Wilderness.

Ironically the promised storm never materialised and the day I spent at Ross Peck's was calm and sunny. Only two hunters were there, Hal Bleyhl and Rabel Burdge from Oregon though Rabel was currently a lecturer at the University of Illinois. He didn't seem to take the hunting too seriously, his failure to shoot anything resulting in some mild self-deprecating jokes rather than the crisis of self-confidence I'd seen in hunters at other camps. That day he and Hal were going fishing rather than hunting, Hal admitting that that was his real passion. Rabel merely said he doubted he'd catch anything. I accompanied them and watched whilst Hal caught eight fish, a mixture of grayling and bull trout, all on spinners. Rabel caught two, and was quite delighted. The scene on the riverbank was peaceful with a beautiful view of the mountains to the west. Whilst I would have found it disturbing not to say upsetting to watch hunters shooting animals I enjoyed relaxing on the river bank watching the graceful curl of the fishing lines arching out over the water, the spinners sparkling in the sunlight, to land with a gentle splash in the river. Every so often a line would go tight and after a few minutes of the rod bucking and the reel spinning a fish would be brought to the bank. My acceptance of fishing, not logical I know, probably stems from my boyhood when I fished myself regularly in the ponds and canals round my home for roach and perch and tench. In my mind, going fishing is part of an idyllic picture of the time when I was discovering the wonders of the natural world. As such the mere thought of it brings pleasure unlike certain other aspects of my upbringing such as school. Indeed watching Hal and Rabel brought back many memories of sitting, rod in hand, by small deep ponds, known locally as pits and with names like Altcar Delph, on the flat central Lancashire plain, watching the world come alive as the early morning sun cut through the mists and woke the ducks and other waterfowl. These were the times in my childhood when I felt most at peace with the world.

The walk had to continue however and the next day I set off again after saying goodbye to Hal and Rubel who were leaving too, though by plane for the USA, and Ross and Deborah whom I left welcoming their next and last clients of the season. Following Ross' advice I looked for and found a steep horse trail beside Grizzly Creek that took me up to timberline and an undulating cross-country traverse high above the creek in and out of steep gullies and across snow-covered hillsides. The high-level snow was dry and cold. There was no question about it now. Winter had come to the Rockies.

Seven caribou approached me, curious as always, and I fired off half a roll of film wishing I had a motordrive so I could take the pictures more quickly. I then descended into deeper snow in the forest, dropping down to Margison Creek which I followed a short way northwestwards before a slipping, clawing scrabble up very steep loose slopes back to the timberline. The clear sky of dawn darkened and a few snow flurries swirled down as clouds began to hide the mountain tops. As I came out of the trees I could see that I'd left the valley too soon; in another mile or so I'd have had a much easier climb. As it was I now had to traverse across the tops of several steep gullies on slippery rocks and unstable soft soil, a task requiring care and concentration. This minor route-finding error brought a reward however when I noticed five shadowy shapes silhouetted on a nearby ridge. The distinctive bulky shape and curving horns told me these were Stone's sheep, a subspecies of the Dall's sheep of the Yukon and Alaska and a near relative of the Bighorn sheep found further south. Found only north of the Peace River this was an animal I had wanted very much to see. Soon afterwards I saw eight more at much closer quarters but unfortunately the light was too poor for photography. As well as the sheep

I saw fourteen caribou and three elk during the day plus several flocks of snow buntings, a bird I was to see every day until the end of the walk from now on.

Also becoming a daily event was finishing in the dark and it was out with the headtorch again as I descended to the Chischa River and the trail to the Stone Safari Outfitters' Sheep Creek Camp which, as Ross had predicted, was closed for the season. I stayed in the main cabin rather than pitching the tent. By 10pm the sky had cleared and the temperature was minus 5 degrees. The scenery had been excellent all day with big peaks to the west. On looking at the map I discovered that these were the peaks of the Battle of Britain and Tower of London ranges, incongruous names that I felt were quite wrong for the area especially when I noted some of the individual mountain names such as Churchill Peak, Yalta Peak and Fusilier Peak. There was a Mount Stalin too but this was the one Ross had told me had been changed to Mount Peck after a burst of anti-Russian feeling. Further south in the Kwadacha Wilderness there was even a Lloyd George Icefield. I also noted the peak named Merchant Taylors, as that was the name of my old school. Still, inappropriate names or not, these were fine mountains. Also Ross had told me that the outfitters often didn't use the names on the maps, some of which were not of local origin but had presumably been concocted by a bureaucrat in a map production office somewhere. Indeed he said that different outfitters might have different names for the same feature, which explained the problems I'd had in interpreting some of the advice outfitters had given me. The Chischa River, for example, was known locally as Sheep Creek, hence the name of the camp.

A caribou stared at me as I opened the cabin door at 7.30am the next morning to find a temperature of minus 7 degrees. Another tough day followed. I was becoming concerned about my feet which the previous day had stayed painfully cold and wet after the first ford and which had taken a long time to warm up during the evening. I noticed that all my toenails had turned black and two of them had fallen off. As I'd managed to dry my boots out in the cabin I stayed on one side of the Chischa River bushwhacking along the bank where the trail crossed it in order to keep my feet dry. A rough trail took me up to a deep side creek I had to cross. Clenching my teeth I removed my boots and socks and crossed in bare feet, arriving shivering on the far side despite the ford lasting less than a minute. A steep climb to above timberline soon warmed me up. A traverse over prickly willow-scrub-covered slopes led to a steep descent to another creek which I followed to its confluence with a bigger creek where I camped on some gravel flats. I knew I was now in the Tetsa River drainage and could reach the Alaska Highway in a day without having to leave the valley. The day had been dull with much high cloud and a hazy sun and the landscape had been bleak and snowy though I'd encountered eight caribou, four elk and two moose plus a flock of ptarmigan. The latter, already in their white winter plumage, along with the rounded pebble-scarred hills reminded me of the Cairngorms of home.

This had probably been the last day I'd go above timberline just as my camp was probably the last wilderness one I'd have as I was beginning to accept that with winter setting in I'd have to walk the last hundred miles to Liard River along the Alaska Highway. For the first and only time on the walk I was camped on snow. I lit a small fire, the last of the walk as it turned out, and sat looking at the black sky and the tiny, brilliant stars, aware for the first time that my great adventure was coming to an end. I felt relieved but also very sad.

I woke at midnight to snow falling. At 7am several inches of dry powder covered the ground and the tent was sagging badly. The temperature inside was minus 6 degrees. Outside the snow fell steadily from iron-grey clouds. As lighting a fire was out of the question, for the only time on the walk I had breakfast inside the tent: oatcakes and vegetable spread washed down with coffee and followed by a handful of trail mix. I was glad I had no high ground to cross between my camp and the highway as the snow continued to fall and the peaks were lost in dark clouds. 'A cold, grey snow-filled day,' I wrote in my journal. I had to ford the first creek eight times in the first hour to avoid small cliffs and patches of muskeg swamp. After that my feet were so painful with cold that I changed to dry socks with plastic bags under and over them in an attempt to warm them up. The edges of the creeks were icy and there was translucent ice on rocks under the water, a phenomenon I'd never seen before, so fords had to be done with great care. After six hours I crossed the North Tetsa River and walked out to the Alaska Highway. My walk through the great wilderness of the northern Rockies had taken three weeks. I'd set off with sixteen days' food yet, because of the generosity of the outfitters and hunters I'd met, I still had six days' worth left. Only due to their help had I been able to succeed. I felt very grateful to them.

The highway was white with ice and snow as I tramped westwards towards Summit Lake Lodge and my next supply box. My feet hurt so much I decided I'd take a lift if anyone came by and would stop and return here the next day. After four miles or so of walking along the road I heard a vehicle behind me and stuck out my thumb. A campavan stopped. Inside was a priest en route for Haines in Alaska. I climbed in beside his friendly, boisterous labrador. Before he set me down at the lodge which was only six miles away he gave me a blessing. My walk through the northern Rockies had been blessed both at the start by Heather at Graham River Farm, and at the end by a priest driving through a blizzard to Alaska. I thought about this but nothing profound emerged.

On leaving the campavan I had a moment of panic when I saw that Summit Lodge was boarded up, but then I noticed a light in the building next door. I knocked on the door. A long-haired, bearded, wild-eyed figure wearing a battered felt hat covered in safety pins looked out at me, a rifle in his hands.

'Oh yeah,' he said, 'there is a box somewhere, come in for a coffee while I look for it. I'm sort of caretaking the lodge which is closed for the winter.' I gratefully entered the warm room. The box was produced after which the occupant went back to cleaning his gun and ignored me apart from the occasional clipped comment. He had a friend there however who was much more communicative and offered to give me a ride to the next motel which was five miles further on. This was useful as I didn't fancy walking there with my huge supply box. Then the gun cleaner leapt into life and phoned the motel, called Rocky Mountain Lodge, to check there was a room and to tell them I was on my way. I left with his friend Ward feeling that my host wasn't being unfriendly but was just not too interested in talking to strangers.

A few minutes down the road in Ward's pick-up and I was sitting in the lodge with a bowl of hot soup and two hot dogs in front of me. I was beginning to realise that finishing the walk was now a real possibility.

Along The Alaska Highway

The Tetsa River to Liard River
20th to 24th October   112 miles

That first evening in the Rocky Mountain Lodge I rang John Bedell as promised to let him know I'd made it.

'I was expecting you to ring about now,' he said, 'and I've just had Ben Gadd on the phone asking if I'd heard from you. You'd better ring him next.' John asked me about the walk and the route and then I phoned Ben.

'We were just beginning to wonder what had happened to you again,' he said and then told me that he and a friend Roy Richards would leave the next day to drive up to the Alaska Highway and join me for the last few days. They were all prepared and had just been waiting for me to ring.

Given the weather I knew that I'd have to stay on the highway for the 112 miles remaining to Liard River and the end of the Rockies. I wasn't equipped to deal with blizzard conditions and I felt it would have been too reckless to go back into the wilderness again. If I did, I feared I might not come out. I didn't mind finishing along the road anyway for the Alaska Highway is not just a highway but one of the most famous and challenging roads in North America if not the world. 'Truly the North's number one roadshow', in the words of a tourist brochure. The highway, which still has a gravel surface for long stretches, was built in nine months in 1942 by American Army Engineers in order to deliver supplies to Alaska, which was under threat from the Japanese. It was the first motorable route to Alaska and since being opened to the public in 1946 it has become a major tourist attraction. The Alaska Highway runs from Dawson Creek to Fairbanks, a distance of 1360 miles and is kept open year round regardless of the weather. For its first 300 miles it stays well to the east of the Rockies but at Fort Nelson it turns west to cut through the northern tip of the mountains before crossing the Liard River and heading north-west into the Yukon. By following the Alaska Highway I would be staying in the heart of the mountains. With its fiftieth anniversary coming up in 1992 the small towns and settlements along the highway are looking forward to a boom in the area's popularity in the next few years. All sorts of people in all types of vehicle have travelled the highway. The year of my walk a party of Italians in Fiat Panda 4x4s had driven down it as part of their Alaska to South America drive. I'd seen some of their vehicles, plastered with sponsors' stickers, in Grande Cache. Soon after the highway was opened to the public a guide to it called *The Milepost* was published as it has been every year since, though now it includes details of other roads to the North. Lodges and other places along the Alaska Highway have always used their mile numbers to describe their locations since the advent of *The Milepost*. Extensive alterations to the route of the highway in places has meant these no longer correspond to the actual distances from Dawson Creek but the old mile numbers are still used with pride. Modern distances in Canada are now given in kilometres anyway. To overcome the confusion current editions of *The Milepost* list both the kilometre distance from Dawson Creek, its equivalent in miles and the old mileage number.

Snow was falling the next morning which didn't stop Sue from the lodge offering to drive me back down the highway to where I'd caught my lift. I left my pack in my room, taking just the bumbag and my cameras. I was back at the lodge after three and a half hours of walking on the snowbound highway with wintery views of Summit Lake and the surrounding peaks. Summit Lake is actually on the crest of the Rockies so for the first time since leaving Mount Robson Provincial Park I was on the west slope of the mountains. Once back at the lodge I spent the evening playing cards with Chris, Sue and Angela from the lodge. Business was slow with very little traffic on the highway due to the weather. Snowploughs and gritters made up most of the vehicles that passed me.

The snow was back with a fierce wind behind it the next day into which I struggled for twenty-seven unpleasant miles. I walked so far because I wanted to reach the next lodge rather than have to camp in the blizzard. The temperature never rose above minus 15 degrees and I walked swathed in all my clothes with a pair of socks pulled over my gloves. There were no views at all and I only stopped twice, once to cower in an outhouse and eat a half-frozen sandwich at deserted 115 Creek Campground and for an hour and a half at the unexpectedly open MacDonald Lodge café, a welcome haven of warmth that I'd been told had closed for the winter. A couple of people asked me what I was doing. 'You must be mad,' was their forthright opinion.

After a nine and a half hour day I reached the Toad River Lodge. I knew I had a room as I'd booked one by phone from Rocky Mountain Lodge, I also wanted to be here as the sub-post office it contains was my last contact point for people in England and it was a long time since I'd heard from home. I was pleased to find several letters there plus a copy of *Odyssey* sent by John Traynor with my first trail report in it and one of my photographs of Mount Assiniboine on the cover. It felt very odd to read my own writings on a walk I was still doing and look at published photographs I'd taken but had never seen before.

The temperature fell to minus 21 degrees overnight and the storm continued unabated. I'd certainly made the right decision not to take a cross-country route to Liard River, I thought, as I plodded head down along the icy highway. Although I was only a few days away from the finish I was feeling fairly despondent and very tired. This mood was lifted during the afternoon when Ben and Roy arrived in Ben's new campavan. They didn't fancy walking that day having had a rough two-day drive in the blizzard, but offered to take my pack onto the next motel and then come back and pick me up at dusk. This seemed an excellent idea to me as the pack was now quite uncomfortable due to the broken hipbelt and I was quite happy not to have to camp as I would have had to otherwise, as the next lodge was too far away to walk to that day. Ben and Roy drove off and I continued walking, faster now without the pack and much happier in the knowledge I had a warm evening to look forward to. By dusk I'd walked twenty three miles and was just thinking I wanted to stop when Ben returned and whisked me off to the J&H Wilderness Ranch, a large lodge frequented by the many truck drivers who use the highway. The owners welcomed me in, having already been told about my walk. It was nice not to have to tell my story again for once. We arranged to stay here the next night as well as it was twenty-one miles from where Ben had picked me up, just right for the next day's walk. 'Don't worry about the cost,' Ben said, 'Your food and rooms for these last days are on me.'

The twenty-one miles passed uneventfully with a few views and more snow. I was not really paying much attention to my surroundings though. My mind was on the finish and returning to civilisation and a 'normal' life. Ben and Roy had visited the Liard Hot Springs and done a little bird watching, that being Roy's passion. They were disappointed with the weather though. This was Roy's first trip this far north and only Ben's second. The weather was bad the first time too, he said.

I had thirty miles left to walk, a long day but I wanted to finish. I set off feeling both elated and worried. Part of me couldn't face returning to an existence where I didn't walk every day and where life was much more complicated and much less immediate. However another voice told me that of course I'd cope, I'd done it before and anyway didn't I want to see friends and family after such a long time away? The elation was due to knowing I was completing the hardest walk I'd ever done and for the first time one that had never been done before. I didn't imagine that many people would care whether anyone had walked the length of the Canadian Rockies or not, but then I hadn't done it for other people, I'd done it for myself.

I was lost in this confused reverie when a battered bus with a smoking stove pipe sticking out of the roof pulled up. A black-bearded man climbed out.

'I've met Ben and Roy,' he said, 'and I've been looking out for you. Come inside and have some coffee and something to eat and tell me all about it. It sounds fantastic.' I ascended the steps and entered Don Falke's home, a backwoods cabin on wheels. I sat down at a small table pushing aside a bundle of papers whilst Don poured out strong coffee from a blackened pot sitting on his wood stove. I was more interested in hearing Don's stories than in telling mine. He was on his way to Texas from Alaska, where he'd been unable to find any work for the winter. Now in his forties, he used to be a travelling rodeo cowboy with bull riding as his speciality. He'd won many events and he showed me his book of cuttings and photographs. Now he only competed occasionally, though he had, he said with pride, won an event in Alaska this last summer. He was also an artist paying his way whilst on the road by carving names and sayings into bracket fungi that he picked off birch trees and selling them in the places he stayed. He gave me a small one with 'Have a Nice Day' on it which he signed on the back. It currently sits on a bookcase in my study-cum-living room, a reminder of a most fascinating and entertaining man.

Ben and Roy joined me for part of the day, Ben tape-recording an interview with me as we walked along, which he hoped might go out on an Edmonton-based radio station for which he did programmes occasionally. He'd told his contacts there about my walk earlier and I'd already phoned them from Hudson Hope. They'd confirmed they'd like to interview me about the walk and had asked me to ring them again when I finished which I did, appearing on a televised radio show in Edmonton on my way home.

After a lunch eaten in the back of Ben's van, the day brightened a little, but I could see black clouds ahead. Finally in the late afternoon I reached the lip of the Liard River valley. Ahead of me lay the low rolling wooded Liard Plateau. I had come to the end of the Rockies. I turned and looked back before starting the final descent. Behind me the last rays of the sun lit up the peaks of the appropriately named Terminal Range. I set off down towards the river and the Liard River bridge where Ben had promised to meet me and take some photographs. The black clouds brought a swift, sharp storm of hail and snow as I began to hurry. The walk was ending as a race. I desperately wanted to reach the bridge whilst there was enough light to take some photographs. The walk became a trot and then a run, an exhilarating rush through the snow in the crisp air. I ran the last two miles non-stop, laughing inside at the ridiculousness of finishing a 1600-mile, four-month walk this way. Then suddenly the large suspension bridge was in view. I saw the tiny figures of Ben and Roy dash out of the lodge on the hill opposite and leap into the van. I was earlier than they'd thought I'd be. I slowed down and walked across the bridge and out of the Rockies. The trip was over.

Afterwards

Ben and Roy had brought a small party of people down from the lodge with them so I faced a welcoming committee as I crossed the bridge. I felt both very emotional and very detached but more than anything very confused. What happened now? I didn't know.

It would be prosaic of course. Aftermaths always are. And so it seemed, as we sat in the Liard River Lodge having a meal. The nicest moment was when Ben presented me with a new copy of *The Handbook* inscribed 'To Chris Townsend, who, having carried a copy of this book on the first end-to-end walk through the Canadian Rockies, needs a new copy! Congratulations'. It was signed by Ben and Cia. Then a friend of Ben's from the Yukon whom he hadn't seen for years and had met here by chance said, 'Do you know it's a full moon, tonight?' On hearing this Ben suggested we should visit the Liard Hot Springs which lay just a short stroll away that night. I must admit that, sitting in the warmth of the lodge feeling tired but relaxed, the idea didn't immediately appeal to me but I was soon persuaded. We were joined by Val Stannard, a photographer from Arizona on her way to Alaska, so it was a party of four that crossed the boardwalks over steaming marshes in the silent night to the changing cubicles. Here, despite the well below freezing temperatures, we changed into swimwear and then padded barefoot across the frozen ground to the hot springs. The water was deliciously warm and we stayed in the springs for more than an hour staring up at the delicate white tracery of frozen condensation and fresh snow on the latticework of branches above. Through racing black clouds the full moon appeared, casting its pale light over the springs. It was a truly magical place and a wonderful way to finish the walk. I lay back watching the moon. I felt content. It had taken 124 days and many unexpected things had happened but I had walked the Canadian Rockies.

Now it was time to go home.

Appendix One: Maps

Ironically I had 1:50,000 topographic maps for the whole route as far as Mount Robson even though, except for the short sections outside the mountain parks, I didn't really need them due to the plethora of trail signs and the detail of the *Trail Guide* plus the two Parks Canada 1:200,000 topo maps for Banff, Kootenay & Yoho National Parks and Jasper National Park and the 1:50,000 Waterton Lakes National Park map – which have trails clearly marked on them – that I carried as well.

I also took 1:250,000 topo maps of the areas outside the parks for the overview they provided. North of Hudson Hope I used these for walking along with the planemetric 1:600,000 Peace–Liard Region Outdoor Recreation Map of British Columbia. These small scale maps allowed fairly accurate navigation in the northern Rockies because of the broad sweep of the topography and because I didn't need to know precisely where I was. Knowing which valley I was in was enough. I would rather have had larger scale maps but my original route was west of my actual one and the 1:50,000 maps I had didn't cover it.

For the Willmore Wilderness Park I used the black and white Alberta Forest Service topographic 1:126,720 Willmore Wilderness Map which was fine once I realised that the locations of the boldly marked trails and campsites were very approximate.

Only between Grande Cache and Tumbler Ridge did I have any serious problems with maps, due to my supply box going astray, as the replacement 1:250,000 Forest Service two-colour map was not detailed enough and was totally out of date regarding roads and trails. This was the one area where 1:50,000 maps were really needed.

Appendix Two: Food

A crucial consideration. Most of the time I live on a wholefood vegetarian diet and I planned my food on this basis though I knew from previous experience that if meat dishes became available when I was either very hungry or totally fed up with dehydrated food I would eat them, as indeed I did frequently during the last half of the walk. There were times when I'd have eaten anything!

The food I bought for the trip was however all vegetarian. The criteria, as on other long trips, were weight, bulk, cooking time, longevity (food bought in June wouldn't be eaten until October), calorie content and palatability, unfortunately in that order. From other walks I knew that around 4000 calories a day would be needed, to be made up mostly from carbohydrates, and that I should be able to keep the weight down to 2lb a day which doesn't sound much until you work out how much is needed for a sixteen-day section.

Most of the food was bought in bulk at Suma Wholefoods in Halifax. The only items I didn't obtain there were sugar, coffee and dried milk, which came from the local supermarket.

Breakfast consisted of 4oz of either muesli or granola with added sugar and dried milk plus several cups of coffee. I found I preferred Suma Super Crunch with apple flakes and carob chips to straightforward muesli but unfortunately had far more of the latter. Either made for a sustaining start to a day.

Lunch consisted of a series of snacks rather than a long break, and for these I had a selection of biscuits, fruit and granola bars and vegetarian spreads. As bread substitutes I had Paterson Oatcakes and Ideal Whole Grain Crispbread with Granose Sandwich Spreads and Tartex Vegetarian Pâtés to spread on them, Lucy Foods Granola Bars (tasty but inclined to crumble in the pack), Ra Bars (my favourite of the cereal bars), Take-Off Carob Bars (rich and filling), Shepherd Boy fruit bars (a little bland but a change from the cereal bars), and Grizzly Bars (chosen for the name—how could I resist it?!) made up the snack bar selection. I had three or four bars per day and ate them whenever I felt like it. More substantial than the bars were the Suma Flapjacks, fruit-flavoured oat biscuits of which I ate one a day for most of the walk. North of Hudson Hope this went up to two a day as I had those from the Grande Cache supply box as well as the planned ones. Suma Tropical Mix, 4oz per day, made up the rest of the daytime menu. I never tired of my snack foods, especially not the Suma Flapjacks which were my favourite food out of everything I took.

The failure in my planning was the evening meal. There was nothing wrong with the calorie content or quality of the meals I took and they weren't chemical-packed concoctions. It was just that I became so fed up with the same mushy texture and uninteresting taste that by the end I was finding them hard to eat and in fact north of Hudson Hope I relied on instant noodles mixed with packet soups rather than the complete meals.

My evening meals started with two packets of Real-Eat Instant Soups (tomato, onion or mulligatawny) to replace lost liquid followed by a dehydrated meal. I had eight varieties of Hera Vegetable meals of which the Cottage Pie, which had instant potato with it, was by far the best, and four varieties of Easy Beans meals. I can't say I really liked any of them, though in fairness I have to say I've tried other dehydrated meals on previous walks and grown tired of them too. I took vegetable stock cubes to improve the flavour of the meals but they didn't help much. I also carried Wholewheat Ramen Noodles which cooked in four minutes and were almost tasteless. They thus became my favourite cooked food because I could add other ingredients like instant soup or stock cubes to them to vary the flavour. Because strong smelling foods are supposed to attract bears I started out with no spices but soon found I had to buy curry and garlic powder to make the meals edible. No, I have to say my evening meals were not, overall, a success!

The above was my standard menu except for the section between Grande Cache and Hudson Hope when I had to rely on local supermarket foods. I tried to duplicate my preplanned menu and, interestingly, found that the breakfasts, based on various brands of granola, and the day snacks, based on granola bars, savoury crackers and tubes of cheese spread, were not as appetising or as filling as my Suma foods (indeed I yearned for the Suma flapjacks!) but that the dinners based on quick-cook packets of macaroni and cheese and various types of Ramen noodles were far superior in taste even though the quality of the contents (mostly white flour and chemicals) was far lower.

Of course I didn't just eat this diet. Whenever I reached a town or café I ate prodigious meals and in the northern section nearly half my food was provided by the outfitters. I found I craved salads and cheese but also sweet things like ice cream and pancakes with maple syrup (the last my favourite café breakfast). I usually left town stops with some cheese, chocolate and other luxuries to be eaten the first few days out.

As I ended up about the same weight as when I started my overall diet must have been about right. I did take a multi-vitamin pill nearly every day (I had 120 pills and the walk lasted 124 days so as I had a few pills left I must have missed a few days!). I took these on the advice of others. I was never ill, so at the very least they did no harm.

Appendix Three: Fitness

Because I'm out in the hills walking, running or skiing as often as possible I'm usually reasonably fit so I've never done any specific training before a long walk. However over the winter of 1987/88 I did weight training two or three times a week at the Sub Two Fitness Centre in Rowlands Gill. The reason was to try and build up my upper body strength (I've got very weak arms) for cross-country skiing rather than for the Rockies walk but it obviously helped ensure I was fit at the start of the trek. Whether I'd have bothered going to a gym if there hadn't been one ten minutes' walk from my home is another matter!

Sub Two offers fitness tests to members and it occurred to me that it would be interesting to find out whether my fitness improved or declined during the walk. I'd always assumed that I ended a long walk fitter than I'd started. This time I hoped to find out whether this was true.

So on the 18th June, four days before the walk started, I took a fitness test that involved pedalling against steadily increasing resistance on a fixed bicycle whilst an electrode clipped to my ear recorded my pulse rate and fed it into a computer mounted between the handlebars into which details of my resting heart rate, weight and age had already been entered. This was to produce a measurement of the actual amount of oxygen used, known as VO2max. The capacity of the body to absorb and utilise oxygen is a good indicator of aerobic fitness. The resulting figure was 55.1 which meant nothing to me but which Nigel Brown, the Sub Two staff member who conducted the test, said meant I was quite fit. At the same time my weight was 11 stone 8½ pounds and my body fat percentage 17%.

Two weeks passed after the walk had finished before I was able to visit the fitness centre for another test. The results when I did so were interesting. The VO2max reading was now 47.6 which Nigel told me meant that, although I was still quite fit, I was slightly less fit than I had been when I started. My weight was just a pound lower and my body fat one per cent higher. Nigel thought there'd probably been some wastage of muscle during the walk but that the fat increase had occurred afterwards, as I admitted I'd been eating vast amounts of food since the walk ended. All in all there was little change, though the indicators were that I was starting to lose my fitness. Nigel's opinion was that I hadn't been resting enough and that I should have had a couple of days off each week at around three-day intervals to allow my body to recover from the effects of the walking. I'd had four days off in the last thirty-nine days of the walk. My own conclusions? If you start a long distance walk fairly fit you'll probably end it in much the same state.

Appendix Four: Books

This is by no means a comprehensive bibliography on the Canadian Rockies but rather a list of those books I read and used in relation to the walk.

Alberta Wilderness Association (editors & publishers), **Willmore Wilderness Park.** A description of the area and its natural history plus some useful information on trails.

Alberta Wilderness Association (editors & publishers), **Eastern Slope Wildlands: Our Living Heritage.** A detailed call for the conservation of areas of the Alberta Rockies not yet protected in parks or wilderness areas such as the lands round Waterton Lakes National Park and the Kakwa River basin.

Dowling, Phil, **The Mountaineers: Famous Climbers of Canada,** Hurtig. Includes accounts of some major ascents in the Rockies. I read it in Grande Cache library.

Gadd, Ben, **The Handbook of the Canadian Rockies,** Corax Press. Definitive and essential. I carried a copy the whole way.

Herrero, Stephen, **Bear Attacks: Their Causes and Avoidance,** Nick Lyons Books. Comprehensive and frightening. I read it on the plane on the way home!

Paquet, Maggie, **The B.C. Parks Explorer,** Whitecap Books. Useful information expecially for remote parks like the Kwadacha Wilderness.

Patton, Brian & Robinson, Bart, **The Canadian Rockies Trail Guide,** Summerthought. Best and most definitive guide to trails in the mountain parks. I carried a copy from Waterton to Jasper.

Pringle, Heather, **A Guide to Waterton Lakes National Park,** Douglas & McIntyre. Useful natural history guide.

Schmidt, Jeremy, **Adventuring in the Rockies,** Sierra Club Books. General guide to the Rockies from New Mexico to the Liard River with an emphasis on backcountry activities. Good source book.

Spring, Vicky & King, Gordon, **95 Hikes in the Canadian Rockies,**

The Mountaineers. Trail guide to Banff, Kootenay & Assiniboine parks, contains some routes not in the Trail Guide.

Taylor, William, **Tracks Across My Trail**, Jasper–Yellowhead Historical Society. The story of pioneer outfitter Donald "Curly" Philips.

Appendix Five: Equipment

I chose my equipment carefully as failure of an item in the remote wilderness could have jeopardised the success of the trip and put me in a very dangerous situation. My criteria were reliability and weight. Although I didn't take the very lightest gear available, feeling it wouldn't last, my basic pack weight of 35lb was lighter than on any previous long walk. It needed to be as I also had 10lb of camera gear, the most I've ever carried.

It was suggested to me both before and during the walk that I could cut the weight by building shelters and living off the land, the 'survival' approach. Whilst I am sure this would be possible (though it's not allowed in the parks) it goes against my philosophy of wilderness values which is based on the minimum impact ethic. I wanted to leave as little mark of my passing as possible, taking and leaving nothing, which meant carrying a comprehensive set of gear.

Pack

I started with a **Karrimor Condor 60-100** as I'd carried an earlier version of this pack with very heavy loads in it on my 1985 Continental Divide Walk and been very pleased with it. However for some reason I could not achieve a comfortable fit with the pack, especially on the hips which after two weeks were bruised and sore.

Feeling I couldn't complete the walk with this pack I changed it after three weeks for a **Lowe Holoflex** external frame pack. This proved supremely comfortable as it had the thickest hipbelt I have ever used. At the same time the flexibility of the frame and the careful design meant that the stability was as good as with an internal frame model and I had no problems with it during cross-country travel in rugged, steep terrain. The pack bag itself was capacious and easily held all my gear. However the durability did not prove as good as the design. The hipbelt is screwed to the frame through a flexible plastic bar which after three months cracked and then snapped in two where the screw passed through it. I managed to patch it up with duct tape but it did not then carry as well and I had to keep replacing the tape. Next, almost at the end of the walk, one of the plastic clips holding the top tension straps in place snapped.

I also carried a **Rock & Run Hipsac** worn in front so that I had access to small frequently-needed items such as map, compass, sunscreen, mini binoculars, lens filters, camera film, bandana etc without having to remove the rucksack.

Tent

Because of the potential threat from bears I did not cook or store food in the tent. However I still needed one in which I could sit out a storm if necessary and in which I could live comfortably for four months. At just 4lb in weight, yet with plenty of room for one inside, the **Phoenix Phreeranger** seemed a good choice and so it proved. Easy to pitch (I could erect it in the dark in about five minutes by the end of the walk) and very stable in high winds with the guys pegged out, the Phreeranger protected me from everything from snow to mosquitos. I used it on eighty nights yet at the end it showed little sign of wear and, amazingly, the groundsheet was still waterproof despite being frequently pitched on stony ground and twig and cone covered forest floors.

Not wanting to have to cook outside in rainy weather I also took with me a sheet of ripstop nylon with grommets at the corners and the middle of each side for guylines made up for me by Craghoppers. When wet I pitched this between trees or boulders as a basic kitchen shelter. It weighed just a pound. As it was often wet it was worth the weight.

Sleeping Bag & Insulation

For the first half of the walk I used a **RAB Micro 300**, at 1lb 6oz the lightest bag available. It proved an excellent summer bag, adequate down to +5°C without clothes being worn. Below that temperature I wore thermal underwear which kept me warm when the temperature dropped to minus 1°C. However I knew that from late August onwards I could expect freezing temperatures most nights so I changed the bag for a **Field & Trek Golden Oriole Expedition** which has a three-season rating. I found however that even in temperatures of minus 10°C I was warm in it with no clothes on and that when the temperature rose above freezing I was too hot and had to partially unzip the bag! And even at minus 10°C I never pulled the hood tight. At 2lb 10oz it is the warmest bag for its weight I've ever used. Between them these two goosedown-filled bags meant I was never cold at night and only rarely too warm. To keep them dry I packed them in a Field & Trek neoprene Sac Liner in the bottom of the pack.

One of the few items I carried that wasn't new for the trip was my **Ultralite Therm-a-Rest** mattress, purchased in 1984 and veteran of the six-month Continental Divide trek and every other trip since. It performed as well as ever and was particularly welcome on some of the gravel tent pads provided in national park backcountry campgrounds. However towards the end of the trip it did spring a leak near the valve which I patched. Afterwards, though, it took longer to inflate and deflate due I think to some of the repair glue partially blocking the valve. Still, over the four years I've had it it's probably been used on 450 or more nights and travelled 6000+ miles—far more than any other item of camping gear I've used.

Kitchen

Because of the need to cook outside I needed a wind-resistant stove and because white gas was all I could guarantee being able to buy along the way, it had to be one that ran on that fuel. The **MSR Whisperlite Internationale** fitted the criteria exactly. It's the lightest pressure stove on the market at just 12oz and has the advantage of running on paraffin and unleaded petrol as well as white gas. Easy to light and run, this tiny stove with its effective aluminium foil windscreen performed faultlessly throughout the walk. Fuel was carried in two litre-size Sigg bottles and a $3/4$-litre MSR bottle which doubled as the fuel tank. I found a litre lasted me ten days and I used ten litres in total. I also carried a maintenance kit for the stove but never needed it, the only maintenance required being to regrease the leather pump plunger, which I did with margarine!

The rest of my kitchen consisted of a litre Field & Trek Lightline pan, a $1/2$-litre stainless steel cup (purchased in the USA) which I used both as a mug and a second pan and which unlike plastic mugs didn't crack or retain flavours, two Lexan plastic spoons, a potgrab (my 15-year-old Trangia one, it's been on every trek), a Field & Trek Waterbag and a litre Nalgene water bottle.

Boots

My estimate of the length of the walk was 1500 miles for which I knew I would need either one pair of traditional heavyweight boots or two pairs of modern lightweights. For the sake of my feet I chose the latter.

For the first half of the walk I used **Hanwag Cross** boots which weigh 3lb and have a Sympatex liner. The latter made the boots very water-resistant until the last few weeks of use when the seams began to split due in part to the boots' being soaked for seventeen days in succession between Jasper and Grande Cache. The split seams were the main reason I stopped wearing them after 800 miles and two months of use as the soles still had plenty of tread left. I found the Cross boots very comfortable for both trail and cross-country use. The boots have a high ankle and I had wondered if this would rub, but in fact its softness prevented this happening and it worked well at keeping dirt and water out.

The second half of the walk was done wearing **Brasher Hillmasters** which weigh just $2^1/4$lb. These boots too proved excellent even in the roughest terrain and whilst carrying the heaviest loads. By the end, the leather was starting to crack in places and the soles were coming off at the toes, but this was after 800 miles of mostly cross-country use and a final month during which they were soaked most of the time and often froze overnight, despite being kept in a stuffsac in the tent. Thawing them out over a campfire was probably why the leather split. Overall they stood up to harsher treatment over more miles than I'd expected. They weren't as waterproof as the Cross boots but they did dry quicker.

Both boots were treated with Sno-seal when they were dry enough and when I remembered, which wasn't often! Neither pair had been worn before the walk.

For camp and town wear plus stream crossings I carried a pair of **Adidas Quasar W** running shoes which I bought in Banff after the sale pair I brought with me proved too narrow.

Clothing

As on previous long treks I used the layer principle for clothing, starting off with shorts and tee-shirt for hot sunny weather. The shorts were **Patagonia Baggies** which are cut for active use and are very comfortable whilst the tee-shirt was one of my dwindling supply of **Rohan Dunova Mesh Cool Ts**, the best 'thermal' underlayer ever made in my view. Both of these garments were used as underwear when the weather grew colder. Over them went a pair of polycotton **Craghoppers Trail Pants** and a **Rohan Dryline T Major** shirt. Polycotton pants are ideal for long walks, being comfortable, windproof and quick drying. Day after day of bushwhacking eventually took its toll on them and they became torn and quite unpresentable! The alternative, though, as I found when bushwhacking in shorts, was to have my legs shredded instead. The T Major shirt with its mesh underarm panels and large front pocket was the best outdoor shirt available. Unfortunately, like the Cool T, it is no longer made.

For cold weather and in camp, where early mornings and late evenings were nearly always chilly, I took an insulated jacket made up for me specially by Craghoppers. This was a standard polycotton Trail Jacket with the hood removed and the inner layer replaced with 80 gram Isodry to give a warm, lightweight and windproof jacket. The polycotton outer meant that the jacket could be worn on windy days without needing another layer on top, very useful in camp when I didn't want too much bulky clothing on whilst cooking and eating. This **Isodry Trail Jacket** was worn at some point almost every day and acted as a pillow every night as well as being used, inside out, as a towel on occasion. At the end of the walk it was still in excellent condition.

As well as the Isodry top I started the walk with a set of **Mountain Equipment Ultrafleece** clothing (pullover and pants) but as I didn't wear them once in the first two weeks I sent them on from Elkford to be picked up again in Grande Cache as I knew that from September onwards the weather would become much colder. I chose Ultrafleece because it is lighter and more wind resistant than other piles and fleeces. The pants in particular were useful for camp wear during the last half of the walk when the temperature, especially early in the morning, was often below freezing. I also wore them for the last week's walking in the Alaska Highway blizzard when the temperature never rose above − 10°C. The top was worn on its own for walking in cool weather and under the Isodry top when it was really cold.

For wet and windy weather I used **Craghoppers Sympatex** clothing. I decided to use Sympatex because previous use had convinced me it was a very durable material as indeed it proved. I started out with another Trail Jacket, this time with the inner layer replaced by a Sympatex drop liner. This was swopped in Jasper for a new **Craghoppers Cloudbreaker** jacket (unavailable at the start of the walk) also in polycotton with a Sympatex drop liner. Both jackets worked well but the fact that it was a purpose-designed waterproof, not an adapted windproof, made the Cloudbreaker the superior of the two, especially in relation to the hood which provided good protection against storms but also allowed me to see all around as it is cut away at the sides and designed to move with your head. It's also the only hood that rolls into the collar I've used that I've liked. In fact the Cloudbreaker is the most comfortable waterproof jacket I've ever worn. And it was waterproof, not a drop of water finding its way in in even the heaviest rain storms. It also protected me against the blizzards of the last week when for one whole day I wore it on top of both the Isodry jacket and the Ultrafleece pullover and both thermal layers to keep warm. Breathability was good, with what little condensation that did appear, usually during steep climbs, dissipating quickly when I stopped working so hard.

The overtrousers were ultralight (11-oz) ones of Tactel/Sympatex with a Pertex drop liner made up specially by Craghoppers. They had full length two-way zips so that I could unzip down to the knee when I started to overheat in them. I found they worked best when worn over polypropylene long johns and this became my legwear on stormy days or when

158

there was much dew or rain-soaked vegetation to wade through.

Spare clothing consisted of **Helly-Hansen Lifa** polypropylene underwear, worn during storms or in camp when it was very cold and for sleeping in in the Micro bag on the chilliest nights. For my head and neck I carried an acrylic bob hat and a **Survival Aids polypropylene Headover**, a combination I find far superior to a balaclava. My hands were protected when necessary by **Bridgedale polypropylene liner gloves** and wool mitts, the two covered by thick socks on the coldest day in the final blizzard.

I started out with three pairs of **Star loopstitch socks** but found that these were too warm on hot days so I bought some thin 50/50 cotton/wool ski socks in Banff. These, unlike the Star socks, were in holes by the end but served their purpose of preventing my feet overheating. I washed socks whenever possible (they were often to be seen drying on my pack) and always kept one clean dry pair for camp wear.

Accessories

For the first time on a long walk I took a walking stick, the **Leki Light Walk**. I've found that when carrying a heavy pack a third leg is invaluable for traversing steep ground, boulder slopes, patches of snow and for fording rivers. Even on the flat I found the stick useful for maintaining rhythm. I also used the stick as a pole for the tarp and as a prop to turn the pack into a backrest. I left it behind in Hudson Hope by mistake and missed it so much that I adopted an aspen pole as a substitute.

Other essential accessories included a **Petzl Zoom Head Torch** (used frequently during the last month when I often walked into the night), a **Gregson First Aid Pack**, forty metres of **Paracord** (for bearbagging my food, pitching the tarp, rigging a washing line and much more), a **Silva Type 4 Compass**, a safety whistle (which worked well for scaring bears!), a plastic toilet trowel (something I think all wilderness travellers should carry), sunscreen, lots of insect repellent and two bandanas (for use as handkerchiefs, pot cleaners, headband etc.). A **Baggins 'Office'** held my Alwych All Weather Cover 8"x5" notebook, pens, airmail paper and envelopes, trail permits and various documents. I carried a small repair kit (ripstop nylon, tube of glue, insulating tape, needle and thread and other odds and ends) and a small wash kit. For observing wildlife, checking the route ahead and whether the dark object just down the trail was a tree stump or a bear I carried **Survival Aids 8x21 mini binoculars** which, unfortunately, I lost whilst bushwhacking when my bumbag zip opened and they fell out without my noticing.

Appendix Six: Photography

This consisted of Pentax LX and Super A SLR bodies, Tokina 24mm, 28–70 zoom and 70–210 zoom lenses, a Tamron FSP 2x converter, a Slik 500G Deluxe tripod and polarising, graduated grey, orange and UV filters. The cameras were carried in Camera Care Systems Standard Warthog Cases with the spare lens in a CCS Small Lens Case. As always the CCS cases protected my camera gear against knocks, rain, snow, dust and general rough treatment. A tiny notebook was used for keeping details of the photographs I took. I kept it together with a pen in a plastic bag in my bumbag.

Film was Fujichrome 50 and 100, mostly the latter, and bought in bulk immediately before the walk so it could be packed in the supply boxes. Between Grande Cache and Hudson Hope I used Ektachrome 100 and 200 bought locally due to the non-arrival of my supply box with the film in it. The results confirmed my preference for Fujichrome. In total I took 3000 transparencies.

This was the most camera equipment I've ever carried on a long walk, a weight of 10lb in all. In particular the tripod was a new item though I had taken one on a week's trip to Iceland in 1985. I would not do without one in future. It enabled me to take low light shots at dawn and dusk, many of which are amongst my favourite images of the walk, and sharp wildlife shots. I was also able to take self-portraits on the trail using the camera self-timer in places where there were no suitable boulders to place the camera on, the method I had used in the past.

My photography on this walk was strongly influenced by Galen Rowell's *Mountain Light* (Century Hutchinson), a book I recommend unreservedly to any aspirant wilderness photographer.